TWIN SOULS

TWIN SOULS

ETERNAL FEMININE, ETERNAL MASCULINE

Patricia Joudry &
Maurie D. Pressman, M.D.

A Patrick Crean Book

Somerville House Publishing
Toronto

Canadian Cataloguing in Publication Data

Joudry, Patricia, 1921-
        Twin souls: eternal feminine and eternal masculine

ISBN 1-895897-04-1 (bound)   ISBN 0-921051-87-5 (pbk.)

1. Interpersonal relations.   2. Soul mates.   3. Sex (Psychology).
I. Pressman, Maurie.   II. Title.

BF1045.I58J6 1993   131   C93-094534-5

Design: Gordon Robertson
Cover art: Sandra Dionisi
Twin Souls sculpture and diagrams: Mirtala
Author photographs: Ellen Tofflemire

Printed in Canada

A Patrick Crean Book

Published by Somerville House Publishing,
a division of Somerville House Books Limited:
3080 Yonge Street, Suite 5000, Toronto, Ontario M4N 3N1

Somerville House Publishing acknowledges the financial assistance of the Ontario Publishing Centre, the Ontario Arts Council, the Ontario Development Corporation and the Department of Communications.

We lovingly dedicate this book to Lucinda Vardey

The authors would like to thank the following authors, publishers and copyright holders for permission to reprint material used herein. Every reasonable effort has been made to ensure that the correct permission to reprint was obtained. Should there be any errors in copyright information, please inform the publisher of same, and a correction will be made in any subsequent editions. Numbers at left are page references.

8 Abraham Maslow from *Toward a Psychology of Being* 2nd ed. Reprinted by permission of Van Nostrand Reinhold, New York.

15 Helena Blavatsky from *Abridgement of the Secret Doctrine*. Reprinted by permission of Theosophical Publishing House, Wheaton, IL.

35 Omraam Mikael Aivanhov from *Love and Sexuality: Complete Works, Part I*. Reprinted by permission of Prosveta, Los Angeles.

68 Anna Kingsford. Reprinted from the Theosophical Society, England.

76 Osbert Burdett from *The Brownings*. Reprinted by permission of Scholarly Press, Inc., St. Clair Shores, MI.

78 Eve Curie from *Madame Curie*. Published by Da Capo, New York.

81 Betty Radice from *The Letters of Abelard and Heloise*. Reprinted by permission of Penguin USA, New York.

85 John Stuart Mill from *The Autobiography of John Stuart Mill*. Published by Columbia University Press, New York.

89 Elizabeth Barrett Browning from *Complete Poetical Works of Elizabeth Barrett Browning*. Published by Houghton Mifflin Company, New York.

92 Francesco Petrarca from *The Soul Conflict with Passsion; Three Dialogues Between Himself vs. Augustine*. Reprinted by permission of Hyperion Press, Westport, CN.

93 Ingaret Giffard from *The Way Things Happen*. Reprinted by permission of William Morrow & Co., New York.

95 Nirodbaran from *Twelve Years with Sri Aurobindo*. Published by Sri Aurobindo Ashram, India.

113 Gary Zukav from *The Seat of the Soul*. Reprinted by permission of Simon and Schuster, New York.

138 Alice Bailey from *From Intellect to Intuition*. Reprinted by permission of Lucis Publishing Co., New York.

CONTENTS

AUTHORS' PREFACE

THIS IS NOT a "channeled" work. It is the work of our own minds, drawing upon intuition, observation, study, and experience. We do not lay claim to contact with a particular entity standing behind us and assuming responsibility for our words. At the same time we believe that all revelation is channeled from a higher source through the intuition of the receptive person.

The ideas presented here are not new. They exist in that vast reservoir of knowledge that we call the Universal Mind. We all tap into it in different ways and different spheres and pass around what we have gleaned for the intuition of others to confirm or deny, according to the view from their place on the Path. All views will be seen as one in the end. The sharing of views, we believe, will hasten the process. If there is truth for you in these pages, your own intuition will be the judge of it.

Patricia Joudry

Maurie Pressman

TWIN SOULS

CHAPTER ONE

THE TWIN SOUL: THE END OF LONELINESS

"Whatever our souls are made of, his and mine are the same. He is more myself than I am! ... I *am* Heathcliff."

So SPEAKS Cathy in *Wuthering Heights,* a twin-soul classic written by a lonely spinster with no apparent experience of love. Emily Brontë's inspiration came from her soul. This same soul knowledge has inspired all the great love stories of literature and opera. Such works endure because their central truth touches the deeply buried truth in all of us: that we are incomplete and there exists somewhere a completing other who will make us whole, as we were whole in the beginning.

In the beginning, the soul, or essential Self, was created whole, both masculine and feminine, reflecting the Father-Mother Creative Spirit. It was breathed forth from the God-source in company with an infinite number of companion souls. These formed a descending arc, dividing progressively into soul-groups. Out of the large soul-groups smaller groups emerged, in continuous division of the One into the many. A long chain of divisions ended in individual souls, each of which split into its opposite halves—the twin souls.

The complications of Creation are made simple for us through the vision of philosophers and poets. The twin-soul story was graphically portrayed by Plato twenty-five centuries ago, in a legend that has caught and held the imagination of the Western world. His famous image is that of the hermaphrodite who is split into two equal and opposite halves, its male and female selves. These are cast apart and thereafter yearn ceaselessly back toward each other. They know that true happiness will lie only in reunion with the missing half. When they find each other long afterward, they are loathe to be out of each other's sight even for a minute, for fear of losing one another again.

It is more than myth. It is the life story of every human being, seeking the twin. Intuitively we know that we are only half. We are incomplete and yearning for wholeness. All of our reaching for love is a seeking for the Other of the soul; every love is a practice for the ultimate coming together at the appointed hour.

This is a significant time in our history. We are settling into a New Age, a new Renaissance—"the age of synthesis," as described by Dr. Roberto Assagioli, an Italian psychiatrist and author of *Psychosynthesis*. We can expect a synthesis of women and men, of East and West, of religion and science, spirit and body, heart and brain. The ancient and the modern are meeting, the ancient teachings appearing in new garb. The idea of the soul's division into opposites is not new. As a principle of Nature, the nineteenth-century philosopher Arthur Schopenhauer described it thus:

> Polarity, or the sundering of a force into its equal and opposite halves, is a fundamental type of all the phenomena of Nature, from the crystal and the magnet to man himself.

Although the twin soul concept has long been known in the quiet walkways of life, it has only now begun to surface in the collective mind. The phrase is on people's lips, a longing is taking form in their hearts. Information (and unfortunately misinformation) are flowing through psychic channels from the various levels of the unseen worlds into this world. Something is seeking our attention. The powerful messages from the Universe come to us when we are ready for them. This message is of love, love that is real, deeper than feeling, love rooted in the soul. It is an idea whose time has come.

In this age we are being shown the scientific face of God. The newly emergent science of the spirit is revealing its relatedness to the discoveries of human science. The love that we speak of is scientific in the true sense. It is identifiable, repeatable, and stands up to the tests and measures that have been applied to it. It is built into the blueprint of Creation and so is inevitable, destined for everyone. It is for you, it is for me, it is for the abandoned on the streets and all who pine in loneliness. Every soul awaits its completion; every life tends toward that, by however circuitous a route. In hidden depths it is the motive from which all motives spring: the drive for return to that which was lost.

The last great loss in the descent was the loss of our twin; the first was the loss of our Original Home, our source in God. The way of return is by way of the twin. When our twin is found, we are ready to take the first major step of the ascent. Though the higher steps are veiled in mist, the love at the base is the seal and the promise of the Divine Love at the top.

Carl Jung said, "The great Architect of the Universe never built a stairway that leads nowhere." The stairway of return leads to the union of all beings. It has its foundation on the ground, in the love of men and women. We are descendants of the Eternal Feminine and Eternal Masculine within the Deity. Through the interaction of these, each new cycle of Creation is brought into being, and a perpetual expansion is achieved. On a long out-breath, the Great Creator pours Itself forth into manifestation; on the in-breath, It returns the perfected Creation to Itself. It rests; then breathes again.

The human race is now on the return journey, the evolutionary arc, the return Home through each soul's pursuit of perfection. The descending arc, or involution, sees the birth of souls. Father-Mother God, activating Its masculine and feminine principles, begins the division of Its One Spirit into the many. In this first birth is established the pattern for the divisions of the ovum-sperm into the many cells of the human embryo. The cosmic law "As above, so below" is effected, and we see that which is in the heights reflected in human manifestation.

Thus the One divides into two, the two into four, the four into eight, in a continuous process by which the Creator pours Itself upon the cosmic ether at high speed, yet with infinite slowness measured against the background of time-to-come. It divides into vast groups, each group harboring a multitude of infant souls. These are the "cells" of the "body" of God, and each is a life in itself. Each is all potential, and every potentiality is fully conceptualized in the mind of God.

As the groups part, they take on their own characteristics. The smaller the group, the more closely do the souls within them cohere. They memorize each other, even in the dim prebirth state. By this memory they will find their way back to each other in the time of ascent, locating their own group, returning in the order of their forthcoming. Inherent in the separation is the reunion. God has taken opposite aspects; but the Transcendent Mind stands above, willing the completion of Itself.

The desire for return will infuse every atom of life through the long journey back to the unity of its beginning. Even in the throes of division the new-forming lives will yearn for the oneness they have known. With the birth of souls comes the birth of loneliness. This is the first consciousness of pain, and it will lead to the high human realization that all pain is in separation, all joy in union.

But the separation does come to an end. We might picture the process by imagining a vast mother spaceship in the air, with smaller ships emerging from it in clusters. As they float toward the earth, the clusters divide into smaller clusters. Then these divide into still smaller groups until, by touchdown on the planet, there is a great mass of single ships.

The mother ship, meanwhile, returns to the heights where it cannot be seen, though its magnetism continues to flow into its offspring. There are invisible threads that will draw them up very slowly. Later, in the greatness of time, they will be drawn up more quickly, aided by their own efforts.

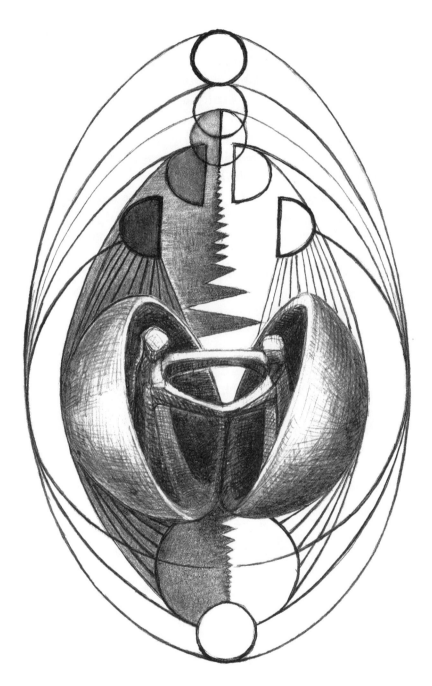

The Evolution of Twin Souls

But now, evolution is only beginning. The single ships (souls) make their way along the ground, groping blindly, seeking they know not what. They seek, but alas, suffer another loss. Once they are firmly established on the earth (at an early stage in the soul's evolution), there comes a last, terrible division: each is struck in two!

These equal and opposite halves are vessels for the Eternal Feminine and Eternal Masculine of the Divine. And so, there is another birth, that of sexual attraction. They now have a direction: back toward each other. Through their eventual reunion they will be lifted up and find their way back Home. But the road ahead is long, and they are scattered far apart. This last division is designed so that the two halves will aid the continuing evolution of the two complementary energies that inform all of Nature. In this, each half must follow a separate course. (See diagram on previous page.)

Despite all distance between them, each holds the memory of the other. The delay in the final division allows the stamp of their individuality to be deeply impressed upon the soul. With the division into opposite genders, they each retain the seed of the other. Thus they dwell in each other at the center, remaining one, even as they commence their growth into two.

Although each half develops separately, every action during the course of their evolution affects the soul of the other by a natural spiritual law, which has been confirmed on the material level. Physicists recently discovered, and were astounded to note, that if a twirl in one electron of a two-electron atom is reversed by external force, the electron twirl of the other is similarly reversed, despite the vastness of the distance between electrons.

A similar energy connects twin souls and governs their influence on each other, wherever in the Universe they may be.

Their evolution is the story of their return and reunion. They assume many forms in their incarnations on earth, passing up through the mineral, vegetable and animal to the human kingdom, where they are embodied according to their innate soul gender. The masculine soul seeks its perfection in a succession of male bodies, and the feminine soul in a succession of female bodies. Through repeated incarnations on the wheel of life they grow into their true identity, the base of which is gender identity. That growth comes about by developing the qualities of their primary gender in balance with the opposite gender, the contra-gender, which is the feminine component within the man and the masculine in the woman. As the fundamental feminine or masculine self grows in strength, the inner opposite unfolds. They are each within each, growing closer as the seed of the other evolves within.

Gender is central to the evolution of the human soul, for it describes the complementary energies of Mother and Father God, which, when joined, uplift and complete. Gender is of the mind and soul, and only secondarily of the body. The body reflects the higher principle. The compelling power of that principle is shown by the sexual drive of the body, the urge of the creative imagination, and the reach of the spirit for transcendence. It is the God-force drawing all life upward toward return.

Earthly incarnations, therefore, will continue until the soul of man has become strongly established in its masculine identity, with its sublimated feminine component evolved to a certain refinement, and the soul of woman has become fully expressive in the feminine person, with a similarly evolved, sublimated masculine self. It is at this stage of growth that the twin souls are drawn to each other, fitting together as perfectly as the yin and yang symbols placed one atop the other.

Today's world, despite all the conflict between the sexes, and perhaps even because of it, is seeing the emergence of many such self-actualized individuals, meaning those in whom the potentialities of the self have become manifest. Psychological studies in this field show that the self-actualized man possesses feminine qualities to a notable extent, and the converse applies to the self-actualized woman. There is emotional and intellectual maturity in these persons, an ability to relate well to the world, and most significantly to the opposite sex. The harmony of their gender-relatedness derives from the evolved level of the contra-gender in each and the stability of the masculine and feminine base on which these are poised in precise balance.

Fully self-actualized persons are advanced souls, twins ready to join or already joined. They are distinguished by the ways in which the yin-in-yang and the yang-in-yin are manifest in their life. Invariably we see a good and flowing and successful adaptation of the contra-gender within the genetically given gender. The sublimated yang, the masculine, within the woman, expresses itself in appropriate assertiveness, such as a willingness to explore, to initiate, to fight for the right in a realistic and creative way. On the other side, the expression of the feminine, the yin, within the man is expressed perhaps as a poetic sensibility, a loving, protective instinct, a mothering activity, as in the professional healer/counselor/teacher, one who does not fear to show tenderness and empathy for others.

These are the qualities found in the twin souls as their lives join. There is high evolution of soul, sufficient to draw them into each other's orbit; yet personal character still requires advancement. Whereas previously they worked alone, they now work together to aid each other's development.

A prime mover in this is their ability to perceive the true being of the other, the "B-cognition," as defined by the American humanist psychologist, Abraham Maslow, in his study of the love relations of self-actualizing people. He writes:

> In B-cognition, the experience or the object is fully attended to, having become for the moment the whole of Being. Since the whole of Being is being perceived, all those laws obtain which would hold if the whole of the cosmos could be encompassed at once....
>
> Concrete perceiving of the whole of the object implies also that it is seen with "care" ... with the sustained attention, the repeated examination that is so necessary for perception of all aspects of the object. The caring minuteness with which a mother will gaze upon her infant again and again, or the lover at his beloved, or the connoisseur at his painting, will surely

produce a more complete perception than the usual casual rubricizing which passes illegitimately for perception. We may expect richness of detail and a many-sided awareness of the object from this kind of absorbed, fascinated, fully attending cognition....

Maslow goes on to say that it is possible in some sense to perceive potentialities that are not yet actual. We will see evidence of this in some of the twin-soul examples given in this book. As the subject of twin souls begins to be openly discussed, soul partners come forward more frequently. A number are now known to the authors and have shared their stories as a contribution to this study.

The meeting between David and Veronica bore some of the signs of the twin-soul reunion. David recalls it in a letter: "... our instinctive recognition of each other, and the way we were carried along as if surrendering to a higher force, words simply tumbling from the lips, extending arms as you did, contrary to your wont..."

Indeed it was contrary to Veronica's custom to embrace a man she had known only for a moment. A well-known artist, she had a certain prickly-pear quality that bristled whenever she was confronted with any anxiety-evoking social other. Like many women, Veronica feared the feminine "softness" that historically has disadvantaged her sex and invited its victimization by aggressive males fixated in lower stages of their evolution. Her own experiences with men had been a reenactment of the age-old pattern, with the result that her defensive mechanism, with its sharp cutting quality, was constantly held before her like a shield. It was a shield against love in all its aspects and could never be struck from her grip; for, like the mythical princess, she could be freed only by love, and love could not get close enough to her to effect the transformation.

But when the love arose from her center, from the connection of her soul with its completing other, the shield slipped easily and naturally from her hand. Through the alchemy of the twin-soul relationship, she made the discovery that in her softness lay her strength. It was revealed not as weakness but as creative openness, receptivity, the very basis of profound and reciprocal love. For as the expressive, tender, and fully generous soul aspect of her yin was freed, she became an instrument of liberation for the partner who was helping to accomplish all of this for her.

David, like Veronica, was successful in his career and presented a strong face to the world. Inwardly, however, he suffered from feelings of inferiority, which made him defer to others less gifted in their mental and spiritual powers. Thus, by cultivating his neurotic inferiority complex, he placed a ceiling on his growth. He had tried to break through it, but his ceiling was like Veronica's shield. It would not yield to force but only to enlightened love and recognition—B-cognition.

Both Veronica and David had been blocked by a gender imbalance. David's overdeveloped yin sensitivity, turned inward to feelings of inadequacy, had created an imbalance with his basic yang self. In Veronica, the yang personality was out front, inhibiting her true feminine expression. Through each of them perceiving and acknowledging the true being of the other, their native gender strengths were released. As Veronica's yin nature was nourished, her cognition of David's true being allowed him to grow to his proper stature. He found his inhibiting self-doubts falling away as his innate male powers were identified, appreciated and affirmed over and over again.

As Maslow puts it: "Repeated B-cognition seems to make the perception richer. The repeated, fascinated experiencing of a face that we love or a painting that we admire makes us like it more, and permits us to see more and more of it in various senses."

He calls this "intra-object richness." It could be thought of as intra-person richness in the case of Veronica and David, a twin pair who perceived the highest and finest in each other, and in the fullness of love, gave expression to the perception. Their exchange of letters reveals their high consciousness of themselves and each other. They indicate the breakthrough from confinement and singleness of soul. She writes to him:

You are so fine and masculine, yet so obedient to my leadership when I lead. I can never push you, but I can lead you with a

fingertip when it is in the right direction, and your high intuition always tells you when that is—and therefore instructs me—
so that you are guiding me even as I guide you. We surrender to
each other with the safety that is born of our deep trust in each
other. Your poetic vision inspires my own. Your image of us
racing up the ladder of evolution now that we are joined,
combined with the fact that we each look up to the other, makes
me see us ascending, step by step, trying to catch up with one
another! That is our joyous prospect of eternity.

David, in his more formal way, articulates his thoughts to her two
years after their meeting (for this state of being was not achieved
immediately):

This function that you have performed in my behalf and that is
matched by the function that I've served for you, the very same
materializing of your latencies, the same encouragement, recognition and nutrition of them, reflects a number of things: for
instance, how we make manifest that which is unmanifest and
bring it forth in God's service and in service to each other. It
manifests also the true twinship between us, because we operate
on a higher than physical realm, while acting physically and
serving physically. We function on a high intellectual realm,
receiving great pleasure from our mutual fertilizations, our
mutual productions, our exchanges with each other in creative
thrust; and this thrust itself is surrounded by an aura of excitement and love, not only for each other but for the world at large.
The high exchange that demonstrates the twinship is manifested
by a thrilling feeling of love for one another, a thrilling feeling of
creative love for our mutual and individual lines of work as they
are enhanced by one another. This brings to mind the image that
in our twinship we are like two trees that stand apart but close
together; we have roots that dig deep in common soil and obtain
nutrition from it, the common soil being our earthly experience,
our immersion in society and in our genetic background. Our

trunks extend straight upward, side by side but separately, and our branches intertwine as we exchange with each other and match with each other and nourish each other; our leaves are extended upward into the stratosphere, to welcome the sun and its energies, receiving from it and spreading forth our own emanations, higher and higher as we ascend. Our growth is in terms of our mutual nourishment. Our trunks grow as we stand in close proximity and exercise our deep perception of each other; our branches intertwine as we exchange, and as we devote ourselves joyously and obediently to the creative work assigned to our souls. This kind of exchange on the high mental level, these mutual stimulations, the love of what we see in each other, reflect and illustrate our twin-soul adventure.

The adventure is enriched by the knowledge of twin soulship, as life itself is enhanced with conscious awareness. Progress toward the twin is aided, as well, if we know what it is we are progressing toward. At the same time we should know that real progress toward the twin comes through our inner work done on ourselves.

That work includes a rigorous adherence to reality, for in this New Age we see a fascinating yet dangerous admixture of revelation and illusion. It is all too easy to slip into the realm of fantasy and begin pursuing a dream. The idea that the twin soul may be hovering near in spirit could cause some to rush to mediums in attempts to "communicate."

One *can* communicate with the twin in spirit, but by way of true spiritual communion. The way is inward, it is between the two, and needs no intermediary. It requires meditative stillness, concentration, control of mind, and an opening to the higher planes of love.

In a conversation with Veronica about the nature of true love, the love of the soul, David attempted to explain: "When we speak together, as you know, we have a deep communion. That is contact soul to soul. It's very different from gazing romantically into each other's eyes. It's a meeting in a more mysterious region, yet it's very real, very deep. It's much beyond language; it's communication that's almost telepathic, like the kind of thing you'd have in the upper realms where there is no language, but there is nevertheless the transmission of knowing. That is soul to soul, and it's an accompaniment of love: there are ways of love that go along with that. I know that I feel them in my heart and solar plexus..."

This is the flow of love energy that courses between twin souls whether or not they are near each other in space or time. The energy exchange can be quickened by conscious attention. Love can be broadcast to the twin and is received and returned. By this means they are drawn nearer to each other and to the point of meeting and completing one another. Beyond this, their completion must await the completion of their individual selves. Only when that is accomplished are the matching halves drawn into each other's orbit to form the completed whole.

It could almost be said that the twin appears on the scene when least needed, when each half-soul has reached its highest point of independence in the divided state. This is also a pinnacle of loneliness. Every man and every woman must climb the mountain alone, and be able to stand firm against the high winds that buffet the elevated soul, striving to bring it down. It is then, out of the mist, that the twin appears, not in response to neediness, yet fulfilling the deepest need of the soul. By the marvelous design of the Divine Planner, the ultimate loneliness of the spirit gives way to the first great joining—and the end of loneliness forever.

This is not like the fall into love. Falling in love generally means that one person becomes lost in the other, abdicating the self and entrusting it into the heart of the beloved. The twin-soul reunion is a descent into the depths of the true Self, where the soul abides.

Following her first few conversations with her twin soul, David, Veronica said to herself in astonishment: "I'm on the edge of falling in love with this man!" That night she had a most telling dream:

I am walking across a narrow footbridge, and it begins to soften all along one edge. I realize I'm going to fall. I look down and see that the fall will be far, and I'm afraid I'll be hurt. Then a voice says, "Don't fall! Jump!" The bridge gives way; I jump and my body remains upright. I'm aware of angelic hands softly beneath me, breaking my fall and guiding me all the way down into what proves to be a great depth. I land lightly on my feet and find I'm holding a book. I open it and discover it is the story of my life.

The greatest fear of the soul is loss of self. In ordinary life, conflict between oneself and others provides the polarity against which the soul struggles on its upward journey. The bridge in Veronica's dream is the bridge that connects twin souls wherever they are. When the point of union with the twin is achieved, self and other become one, and the bridge collapses. But even at this level the ancient fear of self-loss casts its shadow. One must take a leap of faith, a jump off the bridge; only then is one truly in possession of oneself—a state represented by the book in the dream. This union with the twin soul is the model for final immersion in the All, when the soul becomes one with all others and finds itself intact, eternal, and at last fully Self-possessed.

The vision of that ultimate state is held perpetually in the eye of the soul, for the soul knows and remembers its original being before separation. It knows its purpose, which is to return to its origins in a state of perfection.

We have traced the souls' descent from the Ultimate, by means of orderly group division, down to the smallest group—the individual soul—which then divides into twins. In the ascent, the picture is simply reversed. The vast groups of unformed souls, which were the first to leave the Deity, will be the last great group to reassemble in the fullness of consciousness. The last souls to separate—the twin souls—are the first to reunite and will lead the way up. As the twin souls recover their oneness a spiritual power is generated by which they attract to themselves the next pair of twins in the group soul. This will be the pair from which they divided, their "next-of-twin." The next-of-twins may not yet have found each other, but they will be close to joining, for the pace of evolution in near souls approximately matches.

14

The first union aids the second and is followed by an even greater magnetic attraction. Thus the next souls in the group are drawn into the orbit of the four, or two pairs of twins. Progressively the group soul reassembles, gathering in its twins, its broken halves, and speeds toward greater wholeness. All the while, other groups at the same evolutionary stage are following the same pattern. As each group evolves to completion, it joins with more of its level, then with others still higher. The groups unite in the same order from which they separated so long ago. The pain of the separation is the measure of their joy in return.

Joy radiates throughout the Universe as groups gather from worlds beyond our ken and our imagining. We are of them and they of us. We shared the same Home and are returning to it. This is the end of loneliness, the loneliness born of Creation. It is the end of love's longing for itself.

Then the ecstasy that was intimated on earth in its highest moments of love-union becomes the fulfilled promise of the heavens. The Word spoken long before is heard again by the soul, which knows itself as one in a radiant web of transcendent beings absorbed in the bliss of the empyrean, illimitable love.

And finally each may speak with the tongue of the anonymous sixteenth-century monk when God-consciousness broke upon him:

> The heavens are mine, the earth is mine and the nations are mine! Mine are the just, and the sinners are mine; mine are the angels and the Mother of God; all things are mine, God himself is mine and all for me.

This is the high realization that the love of God is not apportioned but is wholly the property of each soul within the reassembled Creation. While partaking of the oneness, none are swallowed or absorbed.

The question has long been posed as to whether or not entering Nirvana means individual annihilation. Helena Blavatsky, founder of Theosophy, addresses this in *The Secret Doctrine*:

To see in Nirvana annihilation amounts to saying of a man plunged in a sound *dreamless* sleep ... that he, too, is annihilated.... Reabsorption is by no means such a "dreamless sleep" but, on the contrary, *absolute* existence, an unconditioned unity, or a state, to describe which human language is absolutely and hopelessly inadequate.... The human mind cannot in its present stage of development ... reach this plane of thought. It totters here, on the brink of incomprehensible Absoluteness and Eternity.

Nor is the individuality ... lost because absorbed. For, however limitless—from a human standpoint—the paranirvanic state, it has yet a limit in Eternity. Once reached, the same monad (Self) will re-emerge therefrom as a still higher being, on a far higher plane, to recommence its cycle of perfected activity ... For it is said in the Sacred Slokas: *"The thread of radiance which is imperishable and dissolves only in Nirvana re-emerges from it in its integrity on the day when the Great Law calls all things back into action."*

In each of us that golden thread of continuous life is the luminous thread of immortal, *impersonal* monadship, on which (the spiritual harvests) of all our earthly lives ... are strung as so many beads—according to the beautiful expression of Vedanta philosophy.

By the same law, the twin souls themselves, long returned to the hermaphroditic state, will forever retain the two unique characters, masculine and feminine, which they evolved in the dim past—our present—two within the one, as the one remains one within the many.

CHAPTER TWO

MAN AND WOMAN: WHO IS TO BLAME?

Veronica writes to David:

As I admire the high functioning of your intuition, with its flow of wisdom, its deep insights and confirmation of goodness, you often reply, "I am only an instrument." My dear David, do not say "only." It is as if I were to go up to the violinist after a marvelous concert and say to his Stradivarius, "Thank you for the glorious sound," and the Strad were to say, "Don't thank me, I'm only an instrument." I salute you, Stradivarius among men!

WHILE AFFIRMING the transmission of the higher spiritual influences through this man, Veronica is well aware of the opposite powers that can seize the mind and control the human instrument. She had previously experienced a disastrous marriage to a man possessed by evil forces. The man had much goodness in him and showed evidence of being an advanced soul. But his emotional being was warped by the legacy of a sadistic father, who had inflicted extreme mental and physical cruelty on him in his youth. This laid him open to unconscious invasion by the dark forces that had cast their shadow over him from childhood. Veronica, who had seen only his positive side in the beginning, was led slowly into a personal hell. She learned the meaning of evil through being married to it, hitting rock bottom, the place from which one has no alternative but to begin the upward journey. In the course of that journey, which was one of awakening for herself and her family, her husband was drawn into the light and released from his possession. This was part of her education in the purposeful Plan for the transfiguration of the world. Now the twin union completed the picture for her. But how is it to be completed for other men and women, everywhere smarting from the wounds of the unceasing war between the sexes?

Completion will be nearer when people come nearer to the realization that all the wars on earth, whether between nations or the sexes, are tangible manifestations of the eternal conflict raging throughout the invisible worlds between the forces of Light and Darkness, or Good and Evil. One provides the impetus for the evolving soul, the other opposes it. One is the will to creativity and life, the other to destruction and death. Both have their purpose in the Divine Plan. Also part of the Plan is that the interplay between them shall become known and understood, and that the Light will gain the upper hand.

The simple principle of good and evil polarities, while accepted philosophically, has still not been recognized in action. It is the triumph of evil that the world still does not recognize what lay behind the criminality of the Hitler era. It is the triumph of evil that people of sound intellect still hold to agnosticism on the grounds that a God of goodness would not permit all the world's pain and suffering.

A triumph of evil peculiar to our time is that feminism has engendered such abiding hostility toward the masculine sex. Women had necessarily to confront their rage, the accumulated rage of centuries. They had been victimized by forces of violence and domination, and men were the instruments of their suffering. Countless men remain instruments for female oppression to this day. But an unrecognized force stands behind them. It has always stood behind and within them. Until that force is detected, it will continue to feed women's rage. Men's counter-anger is stirred in reaction to feminine rage. This reaction has given birth to and stimulated the men's movement. Men's reach for a new definition of identity is an evolutionary step; but the steps on both sides are hobbled by competitive rage and blame. Men are angry because they resent being blamed for everything. The theme of men as victims runs through the literature of the men's movement. Says one leader, "It is time for men to stop accepting the blame for everything that is wrong in the world. There has been a veritable blitzkrieg on the male gender, what amounts to an outright demonization of men and a slander against masculinity."

Behind that demonization are the demons of evil themselves, playing one side against the other. Men and women are maneuvered into opposite teams, each seeking protection from the other. The fact is that each needs protection from the dark forces of anti-love. Men are not the enemies of women; it is the enemies of humanity that have made it seem so. Men are the lovers of women. It will be Love's triumph when men and women combine their power, leading the way toward reunion.

The persecution of women, like the persecution of minorities, is an expression of the dark impulse, an impulse that serves the separation between souls. Forces of unity and separateness battle each other eternally; but the war will not be eternal, for life will win over death. Throughout history the characteristic rage and hatred of the evil forces has found a focus in the female sex. They have employed potentially demonic men through whom to function, thereby bringing those men nearer to the unrelieved satanic state. Motives of power and sadistic sexuality have made women the natural targets for diabolic acts. A rapist is a man with a fiend lodged within his aura, perhaps his very soul. The Mai Lai massacre and the sexual atrocities committed by American soldiers in its thrall expressed the blood-lust of the same dark psychic swarms that engineered the Holocaust and the depravities of ancient Rome.

Yet good men there were and are, and they vastly outnumber the ones whose crimes earn them the spotlight. They, too, are aided and urged on by unseen powers, the members of the spiritual Hierarchy. This is a group of highly evolved beings, known to esoteric literature as Ascended Masters, who watch over the affairs of earth. They are the true delegates and servants of God and are led by the Christ who stands parallel to Buddha, Muhammad, and Moses. It is their mission and their purpose to create an enduring brotherhood and sisterhood of human beings. As they guide humanity in its evolution, they are constantly alert for those who would become disciples and serve from the level of the earth.

Many are doing so, contributing in their own way to the reunion of souls, which occurs on an ascending scale of love. Its earthly base is the love of men and women, leading in time to the twin-soul recovery.

The complementary opposites of masculine and feminine stand distinct from the antagonistic opposites, good and evil. If we picture the globe of the world, we can see the complementarity of male and female as East and West, continually revolving and occupying each other's place. No such meeting occurs between the polar opposites, North and South. By law they repel each other, as do good and evil. It is no accident and no mistake that the agents of upliftment are opposed at every move by powers of darkness, whose given task in the Universe is to divide and separate.

Neither of these is a shapeless force: both are made manifest by individual beings who, in the course of evolution, have arrived at their positions through predilection and conscious choice. In contrast to the spiritual Hierarchy, the work of enmity is carried out by entities on the lower astral and other planes far below, with malicious intent and desires arising out of jealousy, cruelty, and hate. The great body of astral evil that has blackened the name of God was not created by God but by man, through selfish use of the free will granted him by God. Evil is the accumulated effect of wrong personal choices through all of time. It will finally be redeemed, after it has served its purpose in educating the human soul.

Education is its purpose. Although evil is man-made, it has been made with God's knowledge. Compare it with the parent who allows the child to fall, knowing that that is the only way the child will learn to walk. We are being guided onto the Path of return. Suffering serves to show us that we are short of the Path. We evolve through suffering until we learn to evolve through joy.

Yet the suffering itself serves to lift us higher. There is a saying that God writes straight with crooked lines. Evil forms the crooked lines. We are headed for one point, then deflected from it, often with much agony and despair. But the detour brings us round to our destination by another route, and unfailingly we discover that it has brought us to a better place than we had anticipated. The route may be long, the pain prolonged, and the purposes obscured. "How can God let it happen?" is the cry from those who think, perhaps, that they could run the Universe better. "What about the children dying in Africa?" they question.

There are many purposes behind this kind of suffering. One purpose may be to prod human society, through compassion, toward the abolition of famine. We may be certain that there is a karmic purpose for each individual child. Some may be at the end of their earthly chain of incarnations, needing only this last brief experience to complete the soul. Others might be gaining experience for use in the next life. Not a single child is forgotten. Each is as significant in the Universe as the greatest of souls. While we bemoan the loss of life, the higher powers know that there is greater purpose for the incarnating soul than to come into a world where all paths are smoothed and all needs provided. We are not to forget, however, that we still must do everything in our power to contribute to the needy and smooth their paths.

What about the Holocaust and the deaths of six million Jews? One recoils from the thought of karma in this instance. Did they all "deserve" it? Surely not. The likelihood is that their sacrifice was for a great purpose: to show once and for all what can happen when evil is fully and unrestrictedly unleashed. It was the lesson of lessons, awakening us to the awesome power of evil.

The reality of evil is a well-kept secret, guarded by the dark forces themselves; for they thrive on concealment. In contrast, the forces of Light wish always to be known. The power of Light increases as it is brought to consciousness. Darkness loses its power when revealed, for we are then able to see it in action, recognize its purpose, and employ it so that it no longer employs us.

Fascism, racism, and religious wars have all demonstrated how the dark powers foment hatred among human beings. The war between modern feminism and the male gender is another example. This is our present and immediate concern.

Each forward thrust of evolution evokes an equal and opposite reaction from the opposing tide. The liberation of women from ancient repression holds the prospect—indeed the eventual certainty—of improved relations between the sexes. The spirit of the Eternal Feminine will be free to soar and inspire to new heights the Eternal Masculine, the other side of itself. The masculine spirit, also, has long been separated from its true nature, despite apparent male supremacy in the world.

Men have had no real joy in their power, for joy comes through other channels. Men are seeking their joy now, as they struggle toward spirituality. But they are like creatures caught in an oil spill, struggling to be free of the sticky tar, the same tar that blackened their ancestors and continues to blacken the minds of undeveloped individuals today.

The seeds of war were planted early, as far back as the first man and the first woman. From the beginning of human history, men have possessed the power in this world. They did not seize it; it was accorded them in the Plan of things. By his nature, unevolved man was fully yang, aggressive and self-assertive. Thousands of years would elapse before his tempering yin would unfold within him. The undeveloped woman was his total opposite. She was all yin, entirely passive, lacking any of the strength that would later flower to equal and parallel that of her partner. Primitive man and primitive woman were a natural fit, and for a long time the arrangement caused no trouble. They were preoccupied enough with remaining alive.

Civilization advanced and every advance was met with opposition from the mounting wave of evil emanating from the dark psychic pool of the world. Men abused their power and perpetrated cruelties on men and women alike. Men of old are not to be excused for their acts, but neither should the blame be placed on men of today, many of whom are working toward the next step in liberation—the freeing of *all* persons from the down-pulling tide.

If blame there must be, let it be placed where it belongs—at the door of the hidden powers of evil, the forces opposing life and growth, willing the destruction of the world, and dedicated to maintaining and increasing the separateness of souls. Separateness prolongs the life and usefulness of evil entities; the ultimate reunion of all will spell their dissolution. We shall call them the Separatists; for their every impulse is divisive, as opposed to the guiding agencies of Light, ever urging to union.

The Separatists laid the groundwork well for the uprising of women and their demands for equality. Then they delivered their master stroke, which was to fan the flames of women's anger to a place far past the point of usefulness.

The purpose of the feminist movement was the righting of ancient imbalances between the sexes. In a reactive imbalance, men now carry the weight of blame for all of history's crimes and misdemeanors against women; hence their anger. There is the danger that feminism, wrongly used, could go the way of past masculine dominance. Female individual and collective power is now being awakened. Disunity arises when the radical aspect of feminism is carried too far, obscuring the need for men and women to communicate and love and be intimate with each other. Masculinity has paraded as patriarchy in the past. There is the possibility that feminism (not femininity) could become a matriarchy, a patriarchy in disguise.

No person is blameless in the matter of dark inspiration. Influences from the collective shadow seek access through human temptation. They gain entry through the shadow area of temptation, which exists in each individual's unconscious mind. The great challenge that faces us is to withstand such temptation, to understand and recognize the forces that are playing upon us, so that we may reject the lower and embrace the higher.

Freud's discovery of the interior of the mind underscored the fact that early experiences shape and influence later ones. The former function like color filters in front of camera lenses. They do not change the picture; rather, they modify it, lending their affective influence to those experiences that occur later in life. Studies documented by Sigmund Freud, John Bowlby, Margaret Mahler, and many other psychoanalytic investigators, demonstrate that a person's earliest experiences at the mother's breast produce feelings of either optimism or pessimism that will last throughout life. Rings of influence, or shapers, are created in tandem at other crucial developmental periods, notably that of adolescence. Further shapers are continually at work, such as the astronomical and astrological forces, which lend their influence to gravity and to the newly entered individual. Similarly, influences of darkness and light surround us in mutual contention. The shifting light and shadow from these powerful antagonists falls over the rings within rings already coloring the events and the characters, the feelings and the expressions, of every human being.

Yet we are not helpless before these influences. The directing center is the spiritual will, the essential Self, which chooses between the lower and the higher. To make informed choices we need to become familiar with the superordinant, those spiritual realms that have been described in the ancient mysteries and the core religions. Those realms surround us, exchange with us and receive from us. Like stalactite meeting stalagmite, the upper and the lower grow toward each other. The surrounding forces of darkness and light approach each other too, reaching out to draw unto themselves human beings of like mind.

Dark forces are easily attracted to the neurotic and psychotic aspects of the individual. This is because the earlier and more primitive fixations, contained within psychosis and neurosis, come from an earlier and more primitive place in ontogenetic development. That which is more primitive is more selfish and cruel, more divisive, more secretive, more separate and destructive. And so it is that evil forces draw to themselves those with underdeveloped personalities, the proclivities and desires to exercise cruelty and victimize their fellows.

At the far end of the scale, we can discern the satanic power enthroned in the caverns of the psychic underworld, ruling over the Black Lodge. The Black Lodge is that collection of satanic spirits who are opposed to the Light and have directed the massive crimes of history. In the day-to-day course of events, their lesser servants—evil spirits of the lower astral—attach themselves to individuals of every kind, male and female, inspiring acts of child abuse, racial hatred, and the many perversions that cripple the human spirit. In a less noticeable way they invade the minds of intelligent, well-intentioned persons to sow seeds of separatism in every patch of likely soil within the unconscious mind.

It is in the relation between the sexes that the dark force counts its proudest gains, in suffering imposed and evolution delayed; for the realm of love is where it could be most seriously threatened. Any blossoming of love draws the attention of the opposition. If the love is of a high order, the opposition intensifies and continues to intensify until it either wins the day or is vanquished by the force of love itself. The great twin-soul love stories of literature and history (see Chapter Five) all bear the distinguishing mark of violent resistance and attack from family or society. The outcome is clear-cut in every case: there is no middle way; either love or evil triumphs. It is a pattern we watch for in all our love stories, for we see in it the working of a cosmic truth.

Long before Oedipus appeared, the dark spiritual agencies that seek to foster separation recognized love relationships as fertile ground for human conflict. There is scarcely anyone who has not some aspect, stemming from childhood insecurity or trauma, that can be manipulated into hostility toward the sexual partner or the entire opposite gender. At this root the dark forces strike for their avowed purpose: to obstruct the course of love on earth. Love between man and woman is the very basis of human life and the springboard to cosmic union. Schisms created in these vital centers impede the work of the Universe itself.

The deep schism between male and female created by the women's movement was predictable. The higher forces expected it to be transitional, however, and so it will be. But the transition has been slowed by the Separatists, whose tactic is to spread confusion about what constitutes feminine and masculine identity.

The twin union can be realized only between a man complete and certain in his manhood and a woman strong and joyous in her womanhood. What is it to be a woman? What is it to be a man? Are the two simply the same, anatomy aside? The Separatists would have us think so, for to remain in this limbo would nullify the polarity that moves life forward. Alternatively they offer us the simpleminded slogan of divisiveness: Woman is passive, man is aggressive.

Woman was passive long ago, in the early stages of her evolution. She can be wholly passive still, when the shadow influence has her in its grip. But in its developed state, passivity becomes receptivity, that which takes in, gestates, nurtures, brings to birth, and provides a clear channel for the intuition, the direct line to God and creativity itself. It is the yin energy of the Eternal Feminine, and it is not her treasure alone but shared with man. Similarly, the aggressiveness of early man, or man in the shadow, transmutes to creative initiative as he grows into his fuller stature and is revealed in light.

The creative power of the Eternal Masculine resides also in woman, to be employed in her unique way, flowing back to him refined and beautified. These are the conditions of true equality, the kind that need not be fought for; they are built into the soul, needing only to come to recognition and maturity. Such fine distinctions are urged upon us by the guiding forces of Light, while the retrogressive powers work to bind us to the simplistic stereotypes and social myths that breed resentment of those we are fated to greatly love.

To be a woman or to be a man, therefore, is to stand on the ground of our gendered self, allowing it to color the contra-gender within, so that they become as one. A man is yang-based with yin rising; a woman is yin-based with yang rising. They are each within each, and the balances and proportions are the measure of their maturity and gender strength. A truly strong woman is strong in her femininity, as well as in her secondary masculine character; a fully masculine man exhibits all the best of his yang qualities along with yin sensitivities in high degree. When a self-actualized man and self-actualized woman meet and bond, their gender characteristics become shared, flowing in harmonious exchange.

They do not become homogeneous. Male/female energies are separate and distinct; they can be recognized at work within us, and, recognizing them, we can employ them creatively, bringing them into balance and hastening our progress toward the completing union.

In Eastern philosophy yang and yin are defined as follows: yang is the initiating impulse, which divides and delineates; yin is the responsive impulse, which nurtures and reunites. Without yang nothing would come into being; without yin all that comes into being would die. Yang is mental activity in its forceful aspect, yin the imaginative and poetic, exalting the merely mental to the beautiful. Yang goes ahead with things, yin contains things within herself and knows their nature without effort. Yang does, yin is. Yang in his givingness bestows the gifts; yin in her being receives, preserves, enhances, and redistributes them.

Yang constructs, yin instructs; yang implements, yin complements; yang is strength, yin endurance; yang is knowledge, yin the mystery that reveals itself and becomes knowledge. Yang is the discoverer, yin lures toward greater discovery. Yang is the self-developer, inspired by yin, the self-dedicator, for her development and his dedication. Yang is the lover, and therefore beloved; yin is the beloved and the source of love. Yang is will and yin is wisdom, and one without the other is neither, and together they are joy. Yang is as the day, turning into night, and yin the night preceding the day; the one is the force that drives the waves of the ocean forward, the other the force that draws them back so that they may go forward again.

Male and female, yang and yin, are the principles that rule the Universe, demonstrating the separation of a unity into opposites. On the physical level the opposites are experienced as sex. Sex is the ruling force in the world. It is the urge that brings the opposites together to create a vessel for the incoming soul, and thus populates the earth. As a palliative for the loneliness of separation, it rules supreme. And sex is unmatched in the opportunities it offers for the expression of love and of hate. At its finest it allows a glimpse of higher soul states in its ecstatic orgasmic moments. The craving for that ecstasy is what goads the darkened mind in its acts of depravity.

But there comes at last a new balance of forces, a point at which the lower powers begin to lose ground to the higher. People are fond of saying that nothing or no one is all black or white. This is true; it is the condition of our world. But ultimately, in the course of our incarnations, one force gains supremacy over the other. It is boldly stated in saintly beings such as Mother Teresa and Albert Schweitzer, and on the other side, in such as Hitler and Stalin. Thus is depicted the love energy winning or losing the battle for the individual soul.

That separation is paralleled on the inner planes of existence. The struggle begins in the astral, which is closest to the earth. The astral world has several levels, the lowest of which is of near material substance. The inhabitants of the lower astral are those who have held too strongly to the material and selfish pleasures of life, who could not yield them during physical existence and must therefore cling to them for a long time yet. These are the creatures who would inhabit the physical bodies of susceptible persons to continue to play out their selfish motives. Their sexual desires also crave a physical outlet. Many of these individuals have passed over with sadistic impulses unchecked, and they prowl the psychic aura of the earth hunting for suitable human instruments through whom to express themselves.

But other souls, those capable of love, pass quickly to the higher astral after shedding the physical body. In this, the emotional world, the higher emotions become spiritualized and infused with light, while the lower sink from their own weight. Sexuality, the urge for union between gender opposites, continues in transcendent form throughout the heights. Eternally, masculine and feminine will exchange in love and the creative expansion of love that issues from it. In the finer vehicles of the spirit, that which manifested as physical sex finds expression befitting a higher plane.

In the purer stages of the astral, spirit bodies unite in ways more loving and more ecstatic than anything known to mortals. The unions are between male and female souls yearning toward the twin, as they did on earth. This is where the twins find each other if they have not done so in physical life.

They then move as one to the next higher plane, the mental. This is the domain of pure mind. The only emotion remaining is love: mental love, the love of souls, embracing all feelings, purified and ennobled. Here the spirit finds itself clothed in a body of exquisite lightness, sensitivity and power of expression. It is also more substantial, being closer to the Ultimate Reality. The soul is always embodied, but in finer and finer substance with greater capacity for rapture as it ascends.

Union between beings composed of mind-stuff would be bliss uncontainable, were it not that love passes beyond containment into group love. And this is the beginning of the greater reunions lifting toward the transcendental states beyond our conceiving.

How can we know that such states exist? Because flashes of this higher consciousness have always come down to us, transmitted to those advanced persons who are open to receive them. Cosmic consciousness, the direct, existential knowledge of the Divine inclusiveness and bliss of realized union, has consistently descended upon advanced men and women over the centuries. The mystical experience is of this nature. It is also the experience of twin-soul lovers who, by the intensity of their reach, have managed to break through into other dimensions and engage in ecstatic communion while still in their physical bodies, perhaps thousands of miles apart. (See Chapter Six.)

In all of this, evil as we know it is left behind. From the great heights of the spirit, the diabolical force is seen for what it is—a manifestation of cosmic darkness, which came into being with the first stirring of Creation. God willed that there be light, and light came forth from the void, and darkness with it. This was the fundamental duality of polar opposites, which existed thereafter on all planes below.

Then came the division of the Deity into Its complementary opposites, masculine and feminine, and the subsequent reduction of these into the many. The purpose of the cosmic darkness was to aid the return of the myriad forms by opposing it. At the universal level it holds the stars and planets in their orbits, preventing them from rushing back together. At the biological level it maintains the separation between molecules, resisting their attraction and creating solid substance. At the human stage it becomes personalized and demonized, shaped by the desires of individuals evolving into free will. It aids in the application of impersonal karmic law by providing the earned share of suffering for the education of each human soul.

This is the goad that drives life upward. We may understand it better if we picture two duelists fighting their way up a broad staircase in the heavens. One duelist, the Prince of Light, is above the other, The Prince of Darkness. Both are swift, nimble, and full of grace. They are evenly matched.

The Prince of Darkness perpetually jabs the Prince of Light and drives him farther up. Blood is drawn; it pours forth and scatters, its drops congealing into suns, adding brilliance to the scene. The duel is fight, but also play. The fighters play in dead earnest: worlds hang upon their every stroke. They do not tire, though they have been playing from time immemorial.

As they mount the staircase, all life mounts with them. The steps they have climbed stretch endlessly below. How high do they extend above? The summit is veiled in mist; we cannot see.

That same mist floats about the individual human mind as it struggles for clarity in its battle for ascendance. The battles take place in every arena of life. The psychiatrist's office, perhaps, is where the bravest souls dare to confront their personal demons. A psychiatrist describes the following clinical case, a young man being treated for depression. It illustrates the release *from* evil and release *of* evil:

> My patient was about to give up on everything. He had a great desire to reach his spiritual light, but he said there was too much standing in the way. Much of what he said about reaching the light began to sound like canned speech—not that he was insincere. He had long felt overshadowed by his father and inwardly enraged by this. I ventured an interpretation, that perhaps he was

holding on to all this fear, helplessness, and hopelessness in order to subdue his rage, which was the other side of his strength.

My saying that didn't mean a thing to him, but evidences of it kept coming back. I thereupon asked him to beat a pillow. He refused and said he didn't feel like it—a rather common resistance. Meanwhile, I'd said an inner prayer, and felt confident that this was what I had to do. I asked him again, encouraged him, pushed him finally; he struck the pillow again and again and began to feel some anger. I encouraged him further, and he felt more anger. I told him to bite the pillow, and he began to bite it and shake it, almost like an animal. Then he lifted up and said, "I'm embarrassed to show you my full power, my full rage."

I told him that I needed to see it. And he began to fully roar; his face became the face of a demon, absolutely. He faced me with it, his eyes closed, and I felt a moment's fright, a just response to the demonic power that was in him. Nevertheless I knew that both he and I were in control. His rage went on for some time. When it subsided he went into a fetal position and began to suck his thumb.

Out of this came the most important insight, revealing the dominant theme in his life: the inhibition of his rage and strength. With insight came release of power.

In all of this we see that not only do the demonic powers employ the neurosis of the human being, but the human employs the demons, as well. There is an exchange from below to above and above to below. The demonic powers, as long as they are able to operate in darkness, can proliferate. Living in the bowels of the personality they can store up and transmit their poison to the body, the personality body. But when they are released and brought to the light they don't disappear: they join in a dance with the light powers and become alloyed with them. Thus the power for evil becomes transmuted into the power for good.

A raw instinct becomes a sublimation and a service. In the case of the patient, this power was transmuted into ways of contending with the world which were quite beautiful, turning into leadership, into energy for good, into activity and creativity; contending with and subduing the evil forces in the self and the world.

And look! The mist has cleared at the top of the cosmic staircase. The duel has become a dance. As part of the dance the two princes join hands. And now the uppermost prince lifts his brother, once Brother of the Shadow, and enthrones him in light by his side.

CHAPTER THREE

THE TWIN SOUL
IN CONTEXT

W HEN TWIN SOULS MEET there may be an instant recognition, but it is a recognition of souls, rather than an immediate attraction of personalities and physical being, as is the signal for romantic love. Twin-soul love is not romantic; it is spiritual. The two are different, although they hold some things in common.

The initial euphoria of romantic love, or falling in love, is caused by an in-rush of the spirit and the altered consciousness of a higher state. It mirrors the joy of the spiritual union, and for a time all the scenes of the world are bathed in light. But it does not remain, whereas the love of souls who are made as one, separated and then reunited, endures.

Romance is of this earth. It is part of the learning process in this schoolroom, where love's lessons are absorbed slowly and painfully, yet always attended by joy in its varying colors—the incentive to continue the course. Romantic love is possessive. The impulse of the lovers is to shut out the world and to withdraw into exclusive ownership of each other. They are haunted by fear of loss. The cause of that fear may be the knowledge, deeply sensed, that the bonding is not permanent. There are physical and emotional satisfactions, yet the soul remains unsatisfied. In their intense but passing intimacy, the lovers feel the soul's desire for completion. They desperately want this union to be the ultimate one. Hope fights with hopelessness, the result is jealousy and a clinging to the proxy twin, perhaps long beyond the time when the pairing has served its purpose.

Twin souls, on the other hand, have no need to be possessive. Nothing can rob them of each other; what was lost is found, and the high soul is at peace in that knowledge. Far from desiring exclusiveness, their love expands, pouring itself out in gratitude to the Universe. An example is Veronica's remark to David: "When I think of you and say inwardly, 'I love you,' my mind often hesitates at the 'you' and wants only to say, 'I love!'"

Romances are sequential. They often lead to marriage, but if the spouses are not twin souls, adulterous sequential romances may continue; or there may be divorce and remarriage, a pattern of sequential marriages. The impetus behind all this is the yearning for the twin soul; and the yearning continues until it is satisfied. Marriages that endure, in harmony and with fidelity, almost certainly have been contracted between two people who are twin souls, or at least closely linked in the group soul (see Chapter Four).

The reuniting of twin souls is not new to this earth. The principle may have gone unnamed, but we can assume that twin souls have been meeting and marrying ever since the world was old enough to be home to a few advanced souls. Why is the principle being named at this time? Perhaps because there are so many more who are ready to meet, and the speeding up in evolution demands a more conscious awareness of this truth.

The subject of the twinship of souls is very little known. It is not found in books, beyond brief references in Eastern literature. Yet the knowledge has been slowly surfacing in the Universal Mind, finding utterance through selected teachers and prophets. It may have been deliberately withheld by the Guardians of the human race, awaiting our evolution to the necessary level of maturity and responsibility, for the idea brings many challenges. It is fraught with possibilities for fantasy and delusion, for runaway emotions and the abandonment of duty.

Any of these things may happen. Sadly, they will delay the progress of numerous souls. Yet the Universe calculates its risks, and thus has enunciated the principle for us in the straightforward words of the late Bulgarian Master, Omraam Mikhael Aivanhov. He writes in *Love and Sexuality*, Part One:

The Twin-Soul

Every human being has a twin-soul. When man leapt like a spark from the bosom of his Creator he was two in one, and these two parts complemented each other perfectly, each was the other's twin. These two halves became separated, they took different directions, and they have evolved separately. If they come to recognize each other at any point during their evolution, it is because each carries the image of the other in the depth of his being, each has put his seal on the other. Thus, each one carries the image of his twin-soul within. The image may be blurred but it is there. For this reason, everyone who comes on earth has a vague hope that he will meet somewhere a soul who will be everything he needs, and that with this soul he will find indescribable harmony and perfect fusion.

Twin-souls complete each other, no other person in the world can so complete them. Thus, all the beings you have met since the beginning of your multiple incarnations, all the husbands and wives you've had, all the lovers or mistresses, have all left you, because they were not for you. Perhaps you were together for a short while, like a pot with a lid that doesn't match. Whereas two souls whom God has created together are absolutely made one for the other, and nothing can separate them; they have no fear of being separated. In a married couple, when one or the other is afraid that someone may rob him of his partner (and nothing can keep this from happening) it is because that partner was not really the beloved, not the true beloved, the twin-soul. A woman loves a man, he leaves her for another. A man loves a woman, she abandons him ... but twin-souls, on the contrary, recognize each other with absolute certainty and can never leave one another.

The twin souls can never leave one another in the spiritual sense, yet they may have to live apart in physical life following their discovery of one another.

When Aivanhov speaks of husbands and wives leaving each other, he does not mean that this is because one has met the twin soul. If a married person loses a mate, it is because the time has come for each of them to move ahead on the road of life. Most likely their joint karma has been fulfilled. This of course may not be apparent, and there is pain, more so for the one left behind when the partner has found a new love. That love, too, is predestined, as was the marriage.

Even when a marriage is stable, one partner may encounter the twin outside the marriage and maintain a deep soul friendship with the twin, while finding a new balance within the family, with more love to give the family. Twin-soul love does not exclude; it includes. It does not seize; it gives. This derives from its deep and abiding security, the soul-knowledge of permanence. The arrival of the true twin is not designed to break up homes or marriages. At the stage of advancement wherein twinship is achieved there is great care for human and karmic obligations. The twins' concern is not without self-interest; they do not want to risk a misstep that might force them away from each other and keep them apart for another length of time. Since every person and every set of circumstances is unique, the twins are brought together in situations of many kinds. Some may be free to marry, others are not. These can afford to wait, if need be, for the sanctioned time together in this incarnation or beyond.

Meanwhile, the soul of the two separate persons has achieved its first completion, and from the heights of Reality where it dwells showers down its light through the many levels of spiritual existence. Although the twins are incarnate in physical life they possess spiritual bodies of finer and finer substance. Now, having united, they proceed to fulfill their lives on the higher planes to the fullest extent of their reach.

On earth they may be separated by geographical miles, yet they continue to grow in oneness of soul. They meet in the night on spirit levels, in dream life, and, as consciousness expands, in previously inconceivable visionary and transcendent encounters in the higher worlds. They travel to each other in their astral and mental bodies. Their mental powers and love capacities increase, with influences flowing back into their daily life and work. Deprivation spurs the higher mind and soul to vigorous exercise of their gifts. That is the compensation for further and temporary separation.

Why are twin souls drawn together if they cannot be wholly together? Because their reuniting occurs at a precise point in their soul development, wherein each has attained an ideal gender balance and corresponding level of advancement in mind and talents. The event does not wait for the road ahead to be perfectly smooth and clear. Destiny is fulfilled in the moment of its choosing. If, like a parachutist dropped from a plane, one lands on rocks or in the tree-tops, even these will have a purpose in one's life and the lives one touches.

Twin souls are dedicated to others. For twins to find each other they must have reached a stage of evolution in which the will is entirely turned toward service. We may be certain that the great saints and servers of humanity were long ago reunited with the other side of their soul. This may have occurred in a previous lifetime or in the life between incarnations. The other is most certainly watching over and guiding the one who has made the sacrifice of returning once more to serve the world.

There may be many instances wherein one twin is in physical incarnation and the other supporting from higher planes. They may have met and joined in the life beyond and decided that one will incarnate for purposes of their joint karma, as well as a specific act of service. The earthly person accompanied by the spirit twin will most likely have forgotten the compact and connection. Yet there will be no doubt about the soul's leadership in the task he or she has returned to fulfill. Such people will move in an aura of self-reliance, calm, and goodness. They will exhibit intense devotion to their work and probably will be celibate. The completion of their souls will be most evident in the joy they carry within. Joy is the purpose of it all, the beginning and the end: the descent from joy and the return to joy made greater through individuation and conscious knowledge of love.

The twin union is the introduction to evolution through joy. It is the first of the spiritual reunions which will guide the ascent of all the separated groups, returning them to wholeness. None of the higher unions can take place without it. The tip of the inverted pyramid rests on the joined hands of the two who were the last of the group to separate. They must return in the same order. Beneath all the seeming confusion of life is a precise and mathematical Plan. The Plan has been in effect since the dawn of existence, directing the course of blind evolution into the slowly lifting light of consciousness.

With advancement there is acceleration. Momentum is greatly accelerated with the twin joinings. It is the quickened pace of the present age which has brought so many into readiness for the union. Like an advancing wave they will point the way toward full consciousness and the bliss of beginnings. For that, every impulse of Creation is bent toward speed, from the angelic hosts to the springing life of Nature. The desire and the consuming passion at the heart of the cosmos is for return by the most direct route: back to God as the crow flies.

Yet the route to the twin does not at all resemble the flight of the crow. It must follow the way of love's learning and thus meanders through valleys and dense forests, into chill mountain heights strewn with the wreckage of broken hearts and sometimes broken lives. It passes through updrafts of hope and sloughs of despair, interspersed with long barren wastes in which feelingness is put aside as not worth the pain.

Always active is the basic dilemma of the human soul: the conflict between self and other. Self and other have to be attended to in turns, though there is mutual influence at deep levels. Progress toward the twin depends on the evolution of the self; for the twin meeting must be between two independent selves who have achieved a security and wholeness in their own right. The wholeness is due to balance and correct proportion of the complementary gender streams within. And that balance is arrived at through relationships.

We can never consciously know how near we are to the twin joining. The two sides of our development—the relatedness to self and other—have to keep pace. The tension is reduced as we progress, but the conflict is fully resolved only when self *becomes* other in the soul marriage.

Even then the two selves, so long in formation, retain their own distinct character and identity: the soul-self in each, safe within the larger soul of one. The following comes from the sacred literature of the Sufis, the esoteric branch of the Moslem faith.

Out of the original unity of being there is a fragmentation and dispersal of beings, the last stage being the splitting of one soul into two. And consequently love is the search by each half for the other half on earth or in heaven, a search that can become desperate and really painful....

As twin souls are so alike to start with, it seems necessary for them to go their different ways before they can complete each other. Identity and complementarity are the two driving forces and axes of love....

For the complete being there must be a blending of the two. It is therefore in order to develop complementarity that twin souls may be prevented by the powers that be from meeting until they are ready for each other; and also why, if they do meet, it may be so difficult for them to live together. Then the divine planning often makes the outer circumstances an obstacle, causing them by the very frustration they are subjected to, contrasting with the desperate longing to be together, to evolve in consonance by finding their polarity on earth....

Contrariwise, if the angelic consciousness becomes covered over by ego consciousness, one becomes alienated from one's original condition, and then the law of affinity does not apply any longer, in which case one would not even recognize one's twin soul if one met him or her, and the planning generally prevents one from meeting at all....

If they are able to meet one another on the higher planes, that is their salvation, because it completes their love in higher dimensions.

But remember it is a gift, carrying with it the tremendous responsibility of being able to face up to the greatest challenge to which any two human beings could be subjected, and whereby they are graced.

Their great challenge is to bridge the spiritual heights, in which they are joined as one and the life on earth, where they meet as separate human beings. Those destined to join their lives in a close physical relationship find that normal conflicts arise. They are twin souls, not twin persons. They have different psychological backgrounds, a body of divergent influences, habit patterns and expectations. Emotional adjustments are required, as with everyone.

But their conflicts are solved in a unique way. If we look at the Sufi symbol for twin souls we see that the two rings are irrevocably joined; they cannot come apart.

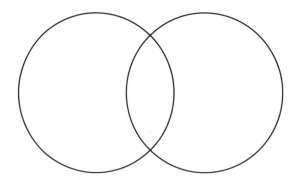

Like the rings, twin souls stand on a ground of sameness at the same time that they exercise individual will and character. The center area, the common ground where the rings cross over, represents the sameness in the twins; the open areas on either side represent the individual selves. The rings are not static, but free to move. They shift easily back and forth as the twins relate to each other. There is a widening or narrowing of the central oneness and of the spaces on each side, where the two selves hold apart, displaying minds and wills of their own.

When they come into conflict the rings fly apart—but only so far. It is no more possible for them to divide than for the sea to withdraw completely from the land.

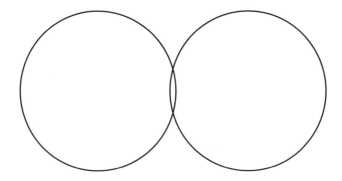

Then the force of nature, which is the force of love, causes them to spring back. They flow into oneness to the limit allowed, which is great but not total: they are forever guaranteed their individual Selves.

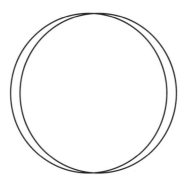

Love surges up in them newly with these climactic events. Each time the pattern repeats their love is made greater. The pattern recurs with the regularity of growth cycles everywhere. For twins the growth is twofold: they grow more into oneness and together grow upward. Their oneness is a process, continually alive and increasing. Their growth is growth into a more illumined Selfhood. It is through the confronting and solving of their emotional conflicts that they make progress. Nothing that arises is left unaddressed; nothing is concealed or distorted to a part-truth; the twins work together on a basis of total honesty. Gradually their conflicts become fewer, and their growth centers around the inner work of each, aided by the other.

Their great strength in all stresses derives from the knowledge that they are twin souls, that they have truly arrived and are matched for eternity. But how can they know this, you may ask? How can they ever be certain? There is no certainty at the beginning, nor perhaps for some time. Doubt has a strong hold on the human mind. When faced with a principle as alluring as twinship, doubt tightens its hold.

How many of us are certain of God? Only those to whom God has been revealed. Thereafter there is no doubt. Awareness of God may come over the soul with crashing suddenness, whereas the certainty of twinship is a more gradual revelation. Nevertheless, events tend to move swiftly at the beginning, just after the meeting, as though to lock the two souls into place. This reality snaps together the two rings, which have always connected them in the heights of the spirit.

Thereafter the twin souls must meet with their tests, which take many forms and add up to the great challenge referred to in the Sufi literature. The proofs of their twinship will accumulate through the process of retreat and coming together symbolized by the interlocking rings. They find again and again that no parting is possible. As they spring back together repeatedly, in heightened love, gratitude and growth, their bond passes through the stages of alchemic purification. Certainty permeates the consciousness—and they know. It is this "whereby they are graced."

The rings are a useful symbol for all love relationships. Conflict between couples who are not twin souls is essentially no different from conflict between couples who are. There is anxiety, fear of loss, fear of hurting and of being hurt. But for those who are not twins, the rings can come completely apart. Suppose, for instance, a woman loves a man and becomes jealous of what she believes is his interest in another woman. In response to her jealousy, he turns cool and retreats. His retreat confirms her suspicions. She does not express these for fear of losing him altogether. The rings are drifting farther apart. The central area of their compatibility narrows. Each goes into the isolation at either side as they try to protect themselves from the hurt of their imaginings. Now the rings can float apart completely, or be wrenched apart by a final outburst of anger. They can return, but the wounds will fester, living on below the surface. Each clash only weakens the fabric of the relationship.

But for twins each clash leads to resolution and firmer union. They survey their fears and hurts, and with mutual understanding, empathy, and compassion, resolve their conflicts. Their built-in tolerance invites exploration, urging direct confrontation of their emotions, painful though they may be. If a twin-soul couple were to meet with the above conflict the true reason for their conflict would likely be uncovered. The woman's jealousy could be a transference from an earlier love, or childhood abandonment, which evokes emotions not sufficiently vented or understood, and thus waiting to return. The man's withdrawal might have its origin in his mother's overprotectiveness, resulting in his fear of being further confined. With the source of their feelings brought to light and mutually revealed, the road to resolution is opened and their love strengthened, instead of weakened.

Twin souls are aided by their gender maturity in the resolution of conflict. When the woman speaks, she is perfectly understood by the man's evolved feminine side; his male standpoint strikes a chord with her inner masculine. Gender and contra-gender have evolved to true balance within them. It is for this they have labored and suffered—though not without joy—through the ages as they followed the lamp bearer, always in front, leading them home.

Men and women of today, though all may not know it, are following that same lamp bearer. His steps and theirs are quickening. It is apparent in the preoccupation with identity, the assertion of women's strengths, and the emergent spirituality in men. Even the clash between the sexes is part of the heightened move toward resolution. If we look at conflict as it occurs between twin souls, their symbolic rings driven apart temporarily, then caught at the place of interlocking and thrown back on each other, we can see that the same design is playing itself out on the world stage. The collective soul of women and the collective soul of men are twins. They are two halves of one spiritual body, complementing each other, seeking their commonality, spurred on and inspired by their differences. Like the twins, they cannot separate, nor can they stagnate in their point of farthest difference. The only possible move is back toward union. The requirement for that move is the working through of yin and yang gender balance within and between individuals. The following case history is a good illustration.

Diane had despaired of ever finding a man with whom she could have a fully loving and equal relationship. She was in her late thirties, extremely attractive and dynamic, with a colorful, authentic personality. She had devoted many years to establishing her own firm in a creative field, and she now ranked at the top. She would have termed herself a feminist; though not militant, she had enough of the prevailing feminist hostility to have collected a bulletin board of cartoons disparaging the male sex.

Diane had been involved in a seven-year love affair with Emanuel, a man who lived overseas. Their relationship was fraught with conflicts, but these were submerged in the waters of the ocean that separated them; the vast distance created longings, and the letters that flew back and forth were filled with passionate declarations of love. Their differences, however, rose quickly on the occasions that they visited each other.

Diane discovered that whenever she stayed at Emanuel's apartment she underwent a remarkable change. Suddenly she was overtaken by a fit of domesticity—cooking, cleaning, beating rugs on the balcony rail alongside other housewives. As the dust blew about her head one day, she asked, "What am I *doing*?" To her complete surprise what she was doing was enjoying herself.

In truth she was expressing her most basic nest-building instinct, her yin nature. This feminine base had been neglected in her years of competing in the world of men. Her yang forces had been in the forefront and created an imbalance and starvation of the complementary feminine energies within her. Yet it was a temporary imbalance, an essential evolution of her masculine side.

In Emanuel's apartment the pendulum was swinging the other way, and yin was claiming its own. But as always when the swings are very wide, it merely created a new imbalance. Her days of domestic bliss among Emanuel's pots and pans always ended in disappointment, for Emanuel, too, was out of kilter on his gender scales. He was ahead in his feminine growth and behind in his masculine strengths. Diane's burgeoning feminine demanded a strong masculine partner to complement and complete it.

The yin force works differently in the man and in the woman (as does the yang, of course). In realized womanhood, yin energy is demonstrated as active/receptive, creative in the highest sense, the pure receptor for the spiritual in-flow. In the less developed woman it is displayed as neediness and a clinging to the male. In the undeveloped male, yin tends toward passivity and weakness, while in the fully matured male it expresses itself as tenderness, empathy, and nurturing. These qualities shine with rare luminosity in the setting of evolved masculine power.

These are what Diane sought and could not find in Emanuel. His passivity and lack of masculine responsiveness roused her anger and finally her contempt. The unraveling of the relationship was long and painful, leaving both of them bewildered, despairing, and blaming the other.

Diane employed her active yang strength to seek recovery and healing. A devout Catholic, she embarked on an intense spiritual search, aided by a courageous investigation of her own psyche and by the habit of well-practiced prayer. She was open, therefore, to the revelatory experiences arising from her close friendship with Veronica, who as we know had found twin-soul fulfillment.

In a letter to Veronica, Diane wrote:

I have not told you of the mystical experience I had after I took you to the airport, following your visit here—the ashram, and then dinner with you and David. I drove down to the lake after seeing you off and walked down a darkened path toward the water. There I stood on a rock as the sun set in the west to my right. I felt nothing except new energy finding its way into me, and then I looked up at the sky to see that it had formed a path from me out over the lake. The sky around was a deep gray, and this path in the clouds was very clear and white and straight. It felt quite biblical—the parting of the ocean—and I walked back in a state of ecstasy and excitement at what I had felt. I had made the soul contact with you and David—obvious to me now, but then I had not made that connection at all spiritually.

Diane later came to believe that she had in fact made connection with two of her group soul. Her warm friendship with Veronica now took on a new dimension, cemented by the twin bond between Veronica and David. Love and kinship cycled amongst the three, and Diane no longer felt alone in her grief and pain over the break with her lover. Again she wrote to Veronica:

Your letters to me, and yours and David's correspondence, which you have generously shared, have been a real help and comfort to me. David, I am sure largely due to your love, is expressing himself with few boundaries, and is thus such an amazing man. His example to men generally will be his biggest gift, I do believe. I have only experienced love through silence and lack of communication—also fear, which usually manages to rise as a block to intimacy. Yes, that's the word, *intimacy*, and I feel more than anything else that that is what we all share, the three of us, that intimacy of spirit and thought, love and the possibilities of all our individual growth. Without intimacy, nothing would have happened between us....

Intimacy does indeed best describe the spiritual union, which is complete at oneness, the spaces of separateness abolished and forgotten. The wider those spaces, the more room there is for competition and dissent, while in the oneness love leaps to itself and becomes the ruling power. Such is the power that infused the three-way friendship, with gain for all three.

Central to Diane's awakened perception was the sense of her feminine nature, her love nature, which had long been stifled, then contorted in its struggle to come into alignment with her masculine side. She closely observed the balance of masculine-feminine in David and Veronica, he strong in masculinity, she strong in femininity, thus complementing each other, while enjoying the compatibility of matched contra-genders at a synchronous high level.

Diane saw that she and Emanuel had initially been attracted to each other because of their strong polarities, her masculine, his feminine, both dominant. But these are opposites that attract, then repel, for they are not the complements. They are the wrong basis for an enduring love relationship, but, in the case of Diane and Emanuel, correct for their required growth experience. Each, with the contra-gender leading, experienced a needed refinement of the inner opposite.

Diane now realized that her feminine nature needed fuller expression. Tentatively she allowed the opening of the soul love that connected her to friends and even to strangers. To her astonishment people, irresistibly attracted to the love energy she radiated, began to stop her on the street to admire the colors she was wearing, or her walk or her smile.

In a short time she changed the focus of her life. She reduced the intensity of her involvement in the business world, undertook further psychological work on herself to clear blocks from the past, and branched into service to the sick and the stressed. The anti-male cartoons were throw away. She rediscovered her relationship with Christ, which manifested through joy and honest pride in her womanhood. Thus her soul became more balanced. She recounts:

In my busy-ness, I had ignored my real thirst for the spiritual, in relating to God and to others. As soon as I had made the decision that God was my priority, my life turned around. I found myself in Paris at a conference to promote awareness between the Eastern European countries, Russia and the West. The Archbishop of the Russian Orthodox Church was a keynote speaker. There was no logical business reason for attending, but my heart wanted to go. I met a man there who had also come from the other side of the world and for the same reason. Sam was a business entrepreneur/arts promoter. We had a lot in common. He had a wonderful mind, and a full understanding of human dilemmas. His clarity of thought and his expansive heart were a rare combination. Sam and I kept in touch by letters and by telephone. I found myself opening to him more and more, becoming intimate. I was ecstatic one day when we shared our favorite prayers by fax! He likened me to a "treasure chest" and thanked me for opening it to him.

When we met again, it was like being with my own self but also with him. It was the first time I had ever felt like this. Now we share our thoughts on God and prayer, emotions and feelings, and all the time I feel safe, held in a light net of love. He is like a member of my family, perhaps better, for there are no expectations, just the knowledge that we are there unconditionally for each other on our spiritual journey. My life has taken on a soft golden glow of love and possibility, of hope, of challenge and of the miraculous. The whole experience has shown me that if I understand who I truly am, and allow this truth to emerge, I attract only that which is appropriate to my path. I feel expanded by Sam's presence in my life. We're not sure we are twin souls, but it is at the very least a close group-soul connection. If it is that, I can be sure that Sam is leading me toward my twin soul and I am leading him toward his.

This is the way the twin is approached, through steady advance in the growth of self and of relatedness. The large step in maturity taken by Diane between her involvement with Emanuel and with Sam was the result of her inner work. The harmonizing of inner feminine and masculine was reflected in a balanced relationship never before experienced. The outer came into being by the creation of the ideal within.

Thus we grow toward realized Selfhood. Our twin, somewhere, moves to meet us in the same manner, step by step, trial by trial, love by love.

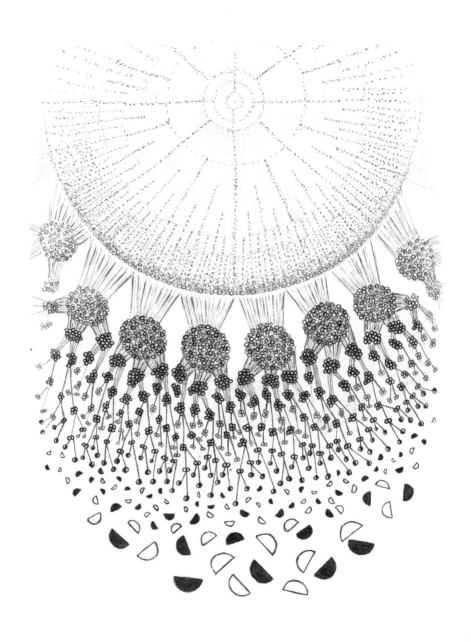

The Division into Group Souls and Twin Souls

CHAPTER FOUR

THE GROUP SOUL

W HY DO we feel an instant affinity with certain individuals? Why are we more at home in some gatherings than others? How is it that when we meet certain people with whom we form a bond we discover we have a friend or two in common?

It is because these people may be true kin, members of the same group soul, familiar to us from ages past. We are connected to multitudinous others in a spiraling series of spiritual links. These are soul groups, each of which has separated from a larger group in a serial subdivision into halves. The original, the largest group, was the Godhead; the smallest, the twin soul. Every group is a oneness unto itself before its division into two. Prior to God's division, it was the One; before the twins were separated they were a single soul. All souls within all groups are twins-to-be. The two pairs of twins that are the last to separate from each other are related in a very close sense; they are next-of-twin. When they meet in human incarnation, the love between them is second only to the love between twins.

Each soul group existed as one for an incalculable span of time on the descending arc of involution. As a wholeness, it possessed a distinct character. That character, though undeveloped, permeated all the embryonic souls within it. The uniqueness of the group is forever reflected in those individuals whose formative prebirth occurred in its embrace. One group, for instance, might be identified as the soul of music, another of artistry, of science, invention, or healing. In the womb of the cosmos the gifts were assigned. The recipients were to develop them in their unique way.

Though all groups have cohered for infinitely long periods, some have been held together longer than others. The smaller the groups, or the later in separating, the longer the soul-cells within them will have nestled together, absorbing, exchanging, familiarizing themselves with the specks of life that will develop into the kindred souls of human existence.

We speak of "our group soul," but finally there is no separate group to which we belong. We belong to all, for we have been a part of every group on the long descent from the One. Our spiritual closeness to others around us is relative and founded on the sequence of separation. Thus the greatest closeness is to our twin soul, then our next-of-twin, and our next and next again, similar to family relationships: siblings, cousins, second cousins, third cousins, and so on. Though there are groups near us and groups far, we are in truth one soul. Ultimately we will be gathered together in a great family reunion, at which time there will be no distance between any one and another. Hierarchies, orders of descent and ascent, will have passed away, and every soul will be the beloved of every other.

This is the end point to which all life is moving. The detours and setbacks are part of the duel and the dance between the Princes of Light and Darkness, a duel that serves to speed the ascension and return. The descent was by the will of God; the ascent is by the will of the individual souls, which have become infused with the will of God. Unconsciously they departed from the One; in consciousness they return.

Consciousness of the Plan and its purpose has been surfacing in our enlightened time. We witness a gathering of groups the world over, with dedication to humanitarianism, spiritual awakening, and concern for the planetary body, all of which is evidence of group souls reaching to each other and to those less advanced on the scale. It is synchronous with the drawing together of twin souls in significant numbers—necessarily so, for it is the twins who must lead the way up.

Twin souls are approaching each other in every country of the world and in worlds beyond our own, across the vastness of time and the cosmos. They stand at the center of groups that extend around and beyond them, in circles expanding and overlapping, the outer awaiting the approach of the inner, the higher urging and aiding the rise of the lower. The process has been going on for aeons. Many who have gone before have reached pinnacles of achievement in the higher worlds, and from there they aid our return.

Through the magnetism of their union, twin souls attract to themselves those who belong to their near group. Meanwhile, the groups are collecting. At the same time as people are preparing themselves individually, they are creating bonds with those for whom they feel a deep kinship.

Let us look, for example, at the companionship of four women whose lives have blended in the manner of a group soul rediscovering itself. Margaret, Hilda, Violet and Fran have maintained a close and enduring friendship for some years, with the commonality of interest and sympathetic understanding characteristic of soul kinship. They are all on the spiritual path, and each is in a work of service, though by way of different occupations. None has encountered her twin soul, but they are acquainted with the principle and are aware of moving in that direction. They know that the direction is that of individual growth, and they pursue this in many ways, one of which is co-counseling.

Says Margaret, "I feel I'm not ready for my twin soul as yet. I feel the gaps in my learning. I have work to do." Part of her work, though she does not state it, is to resolve her faint yet lingering hostility toward men.

She has a good understanding of the group soul and senses that she and her friends are spiritually related. Of their relative placement in the group, she says, "I'm closest to Hilda, not quite so close to Violet, and a touch farther from Fran." Some might view these as emotional distinctions, and that would be partly true. But the emotions tend to follow the direction of the spirit, and it is likely that Margaret was perceiving at soul level the ancient pattern of the group.

The four women have been very much affected by one another. They sometimes had matching dreams on the same night, sometimes precognitive glimpses of what lies ahead for one another. They have a sense of fulfilling a group purpose, the pooling of experience, so that the progress of one contributes to the knowledge and progress of the others. Violet, for instance, began to take lessons in t'ai chi. When Fran joined the group six months later, she found the chi energy radiating through her almost at once, without the many months of exercise preparation.

The group sharing is a cosmic time-saver. Every soul must partake of all experience, but this plan teaches us that all the burdens need not be assumed individually. As the group souls fuse in harmony, the experience of every soul flows into the others and becomes their own. In the end, each will be all-knowing without having had to drink every cup to the bottom.

Thus group love expresses itself. The movements of groups and of the constituent inner souls toward each other are expressions of higher love. This is the joy in the ascent. As we encounter those of our group in this lifetime and quickly grow to love them, we find that the love has a different quality from the affections and passions we have known before. It is the conscious realization of soul love. All love is of the soul, but oftentimes dimmed by the filters of the lower emotions, with their pains and precarious joys, their mad swings between opposites. In group-soul love we find true compatibility. The recognition that we share is an echo of ancient togetherness. There is a contiguity, established in the predawn of consciousness. Now, after a long time of growing, we stand together on the mountain of evolution at almost the same place. Only the twins may occupy the same place exactly. Twins are two sides of the same soul, whereas those of the group, though related, are separate. In the twins there is sameness, in the group similarity. But the similarities are profound. Finding another who sees things just as we do is everyone's dream of friendship.

Group-soul love springs from a deep well. It comes to us already matured, by virtue of the prolonged connection. The best marriages are founded on enduring love and compatibility, accompanied with a matching rate of growth. These are marriages between members of a group soul. The closer they stand in the group, the deeper their bond.

A marriage between two people who are next-of-twin is surpassed only by one between twin souls. The twin-soul marriage remains relatively rare, though it will occur much more in this advancing New Age. By the close of it, and perhaps earlier, the twin-soul marriage may be the rule rather than the exception. Then indeed the earth will be the paradise of its foretelling.

Married couples who appear to be worlds apart in fact probably are in a sense. They are from soul groups far apart in the schematic design. But they have been brought together as purposefully as the twins and group lovers, paired not for the joy of union but for karmic learning. Ascendence does not occur in easy stages but only after long preparation. Those who meet simply and easily in twin or group-soul love have struggled toward each other through many vicissitudes. They have reached through the spaces and met in tangled heaps long before they were ready; for this is how readiness comes.

The earthly family is a preparatory ground, sometimes a battleground, for the souls' learning. It is a run-through for the group-soul union, a sort of practice at getting along. Individuals in a family often seem to be at varying levels of evolution. We may be sure that this is an ordained imbalance of soul strengths, the more developed individuals being intended to lift the lesser.

Do the genetic family and the soul family coincide? Not generally. With advanced evolution, however, the soul can choose its human family before incarnating; thus it can happen that two or more from a group soul are born into the same earthly family. Such a gift comes with its own share of difficulties. Perhaps one parent and one child are from the same group soul, which results in the two having a special bond; this may generate feelings of jealousy and reactive guilt among the others. There is almost always some favoritism in a family, with the attendant pain and guilt. If only people could know that the basic reason for their fondnesses is the positioning of their soul in the tapestry of the heavens!

At the other end of the scale from the gifted family, is the one that seems to consist of souls from different universes. Here there is intolerable conflict and tension, the very antithesis of the empathic understanding that comes naturally to those in a near group. The dark forces capitalize on the strife, and there can be lives of misery, producing drug and alcohol addictions, child abuse, wife battering, suicide, and murder. These are souls with grave karmic debts to pay and, tragically, new ones mounting up. Conversely, the people who relate in harmony remain open to the spiritual light, and in the course of their lives build good karma for themselves This is one application of the biblical saying, "To him who hath shall be given, and from him who hath not shall be taken away even that which he hath."

It may be that those whose lives seem cursed instead of blessed are souls whose evolution is being forced. Perhaps they have been resistant to their growth. We evolve willingly or by force, a choice that the Universe allows. If we are not willing, our evolution is forced upon us, and comes with the sorrow and tragedy that will wake us up. At the same time we can know that every individual is of the same divine lineage as everyone else and is regarded as sacred by the lords of karma, who bring all arrangements into being and into perfect balance on the scales of justice.

The work of the great beings is to facilitate the upward-reaching life. The impulse of all that has been created is toward union, whatever the pace may be. All groups, clubs, organizations, and collectives are following the inner summons to cohere and return. Their activities accord with the strengthening will to goodness throughout evolving life. Groups with an altruistic purpose are a feature of the later centuries, ours especially: the Salvation Army, the Theosophical Society, the Humane Society, Red Cross, Alcoholics Anonymous, and countless others.

They have their evil counterparts. Neo-Nazis, white supremacists, and international terrorist organizations also obey the call to union. But their union is to further the cause of separation. Powers of darkness work best by luring the soul in the direction of its fundamental drives and then distorting these drives. As an example, the altruistic principle of communism was seized and utilized by demonic forces to serve a power-hungry oligarchy. Yet the fate of communism shows again that the victories of Darkness will not endure. They are temporary, but can exert great power in their time. The pages of history are blackened by such evils as the Inquisition, the Mongolian terror under Genghis Khan, the Stalin purges.

Devastating as these times were, their effect on the world has faded, while the workings of the light live among us through the generations. The darkness has its day and passes; it is not of the evolving stream. The ascension and assembly of group souls render steady illumination to the human scene. Proof of this is the tremendous group displays of service to humanity throughout the centuries. Advanced group souls have periodically descended into incarnation to elevate the race with quantum leaps in art or science, or to feed the thirsting soul of humanity with music, the direct voice of God.

Group identity clearly revealed itself with the touching down of the great composers, giants such as Bach, Haydn, Beethoven, Mozart, and Brahms. They and others of their soul group rendered a gift of musical creation the like of which the world has never known. And then, there was the collective soul of the master painters: Leonardo da Vinci, Michelangelo, Raphael, and others, all of whom came into incarnation within a brief time of each other. In the gift of their creations, these greats illustrated the return of like to like in the advanced group soul.

So, too, did the great thinkers, another highly evolved group soul who elected to incarnate and open the world of science to a blind and groping humanity. It required some time for the revelations of Copernicus and Galileo to be absorbed, but the pace accelerated with the arrival of Darwin, Newton, and Einstein. Newton, probably the greatest of them, hardly entered into human life at all, but merely stood apart, contributing. He mirrors his lost heaven in these words, written shortly before his death: "I do not know what I may appear to the world, but to myself I seem to have been only like a boy playing on the seashore and diverting myself in now and then finding a smoother pebble or a prettier shell than ordinary, whilst the great ocean of truth lay all undiscovered before me."

The group soul of psychology brought to our midst another wave of like souls, spearheaded by Freud and followed by such greats as Jung, Adler and Reich. Because they are closer to us in time, we are aware of dissonances and jealousies amongst these kindred souls. For instance, Jung was Freud's announced heir apparent, his undisputed favorite. But when Jung eventually diverged from his mentor, Freud, instead of accepting the difference of viewpoint, reacted so strongly that it led to a major schism. Jung followed his own path, which Freud called "too religious." Jung, in turn, judged Freud autocratic and closedminded. The truths of their separate visions were from a high plane, the causes for the parting from a lesser-evolved level.

We see intimations of such anger and jealousy in the lives of the towering composers, painters, and scientists. It lets us know that our human foibles will not automatically pass away as we join our group. Union is a process, not an instant occurrence. The same is true for twin-soul unions. There is much creative work to do in the melding of strong souls, who must learn to maintain individuality while moving toward oneness.

The joining of group souls is similar to the creative apposition of words by the writer, or of musical notes by the composer. Souls, words, notes belong together in a certain order and combination. It is the task of the creator to make the right connections.

But what about homosexuality? Where does this group, which now clubs together and has for so long been cast out from society, fit into the group-soul concept? Most certainly it occupies a rightful place in the Grand Plan for the ongoing development of gender and contra-gender. Homosexuality should be viewed against the backdrop of the extended life of the soul and of the group soul. The need of the group soul is to develop all aspects of itself during its evolution to wholeness. Collectively it must achieve a perfect balance of masculine and feminine components, as must each soul within the group.

For this purpose each member soul has elected to take different paths in its serial incarnations. The homosexual path has been taken as choice by many of the greats: Michelangelo, Walt Whitman, and Edward Carpenter, all three cosmic conscious illuminates. Walt Whitman and Edward Carpenter, both poets, were closely linked in their group soul, not as lovers but through the soul-love saturation of their poems. They incarnated contemporaneously: Carpenter in England and Whitman in America, later to meet as famous men. Here we see a group-soul pattern, lives of service, not only to this world but to the soul of literature to which they belonged.

Both men showed a high advancement of their inner masculine and feminine portions. In each, the forceful creative power of the yang was well balanced with the yin sensitivities. They did not seek their twin souls in their lifetimes. Perhaps the twin had already been joined in a former incarnation and was standing by while this half of the soul chose to leave their completion in order to give further service and shed more light on this world.

In homosexuality we see a combination of gender and contra-gender, just as in heterosexuality. The Eternal Feminine and Eternal Masculine attributes of the soul find love expression in whatever circumstances the life-map decrees. The old idea that man is man and woman is woman no longer holds. Each of us is both, and we remain both when the spirit escapes in sleep or when we leave this earthly coil.

Men who love men are giving creative expression to the same dual energies. It is not that one is the female of the pair and the other the male. Their personalities may complement each other through the higher yin level in the one and the higher yang in the other. The same is true of lesbians. Yin and yang may shift and change as they do between any man and any woman released from inner restrictions, the man being allowed his passivity, the woman her assertiveness. The aim of gender unfoldment is to liberate the complementary energies so that they can flow in free exchange within the person and between two persons, and finally among all persons and souls.

Why cannot two men be twin souls, or two women? is a question sometimes asked.

There can be great love and creative collaboration between homosexual couples, particularly those linked closely in the group soul. But with gender sameness, the polarities are missing. It is the polarity of positive and negative that gives us electricity and powers our brains. Polarity is the nature of the created Universe. The unit we call the twin soul is a universe in miniature and is necessarily founded on opposite genders, the Eternal Feminine and Eternal Masculine. The purpose of its division into halves is to evolve God's complementary energies and return them to wholeness in the microcosm of the twins and the macrocosm of the All.

If we accept homosexuality in a particular lifetime as a necessary episode in the growth of the oversoul, we still have a question: what about the psychological factors that operate within the present life? The answer may be that these are active and meshed with deeper influences, as it true in everything else. The concept of archetypes, as defined by Carl Jung, informs us that these influences—the feminine archetype, the masculine archetype, the maternal and the hero archetypes, and so on—are operating over us, as well as within us, from the time of conception. They alone do not shape the individual, but combine with the psychological influences present throughout the life of a person. The mission of the soul in this lifetime, as defined from above, interplays with the major influences in the human life. An example is the intimidating father whose behavior reinforces the tendency to homosexuality in the male child. Psychoanalytic researches have shown that during the Oedipal period, when the child is four or five, if the father is too frightening, the child will slip back into an earlier period. He will identify with the mother and say, in effect, through the course of his development, "Don't be afraid of me as a competitor. I'm only a woman who wants to love you."

Such an event would not necessarily be a defection of the overarching plan for gender and contra-gender combination in the life, but would mesh with the grand design for the long-term mission of the soul.

Lacking knowledge of gender composition, some are convinced

they have been born into the wrong body. But the Universe does not make mistakes. The right sex is always clothed in the right body, the masculine side of the soul in a man's body and the feminine in a woman's.

A man, for instance may feel very feminine and yearn for the outward form, the grace, the gentle and flowing movements associated with the female body to match his feeling. He cannot know that his soul, before birth, chose the life situation specifically for raising the level of his yin aspect. He may in a past life have devoted himself very strongly to his yang—as a warrior, perhaps—and now needs the compensating balance. Our gender growth goes through stages, like our evolution toward self and other, with emphasis on one, then the other, then back again. In the extreme case, in which an attempt is made to change one's sex surgically, one is flying in the face of the cosmic Plan.

A woman, too, may feel inwardly that she is male and has been mistakenly cast into the wrong mold. This opinion is strengthened if a psychic tells her that she was a man in a previous life. Interestingly, many women are given this message, but few men are told they were women in former lives.

Mediums, psychics, and other sensitives are more open than others to the influence of mass thought-forms. One powerful thought-form, long existent in the astral realm, is that we alternate sexes in our successive incarnations. The reason given is that the soul needs the experience of both sexes. It is true that the soul needs that experience, but the twin-soul principle provides another explanation. If every soul were complete in itself it might be required to go through a roulette spin of sex changes. But with twin soulship the experience of both sexes is acquired in shared fashion by the twins. At their initial division into two halves, each of the twin souls retains a part of the other's essence. Their incarnations as rudimentary male and female creatures follow the very early division of the sexes in Nature. During successive lives they evolve their basic selves, as well as the portion of the other, the contra-gender, that they carry within. In a small but vital way, the male experience enters the female soul, and her experience enters his. The twin souls are forever joined at their center, however far apart they may be in space. The feminine soul clothes itself in myriad female forms through age after age of slow growth. Every development of the feminine nature is absorbed by the masculine counterpart. As gender advances in both, the contra-gender similarly grows, gaining in balance. The plan is that they shall learn of each other by becoming built into each other, as they once were whole in the unconscious state. It is for growth into consciousness and experience in material form that they are parted and are now rejoining. They have no need to alternate their sexes in earthly life. As they evolve into self-definition she could say, "I, woman, know what it is to be man, without need of the body parts; I know it as my own inner masculine takes on strength and fortitude, creative initiative and leadership." He could say, "I, man, have knowledge of womanliness as my womanliness expands my heart from within, inspires my higher mind and stirs my most compassionate and tender feelings toward the young and the needful all about me."

When at last they find each other, they are able to re-establish their oneness, because they have become one in developed soul substance. The part of the male that has grown to completion in the female soul is a part of her being, as is the extension of herself residing in him. This explains why Cathy, in *Wuthering Heights,* can say in truth, "I *am* Heathcliff!"

The same situation prevails to a degree among souls in the group. They share a soul substance, comparable with the genes in a family. As they grow closer, that substance expands within each. They grow individually, becoming more and more themselves, and also becoming more and more each other.

This is how the experience of one becomes the experience of all. In the higher stages of group joining, all boundaries are dissolved. Everything that each soul has experienced becomes common property, a gift to the others. Yet at the same time, all that makes each soul a unique self persists and intensifies.

A question often asked about the crippled, the blind, and the severely handicapped is: "Are they paying the karmic price for crimes of the past?" That would describe karma in a narrow sense and we, your authors, believe, wrongly.

The fact is that all things, including painful ones, must be brought to general consciousness for the collective soul of humanity to realize itself. It must learn of its capacities, its power of compassion, of endurance, adaptation, inventiveness, and givingness, together adding up to its growth in love. Each soul finally has to know all things from the center, that is, by experience. The group sharing helps us to speed this process. The group soul divides; each member chooses its portion for the life ahead. The heavy burdens in life are always borne by developed souls; they are not given to the young ones. As the group members prepare to descend into human existence, the strongest will select the least welcome tasks. Why else would Down Syndrome children, the cerebral palsied, the Helen Kellers, radiate such great and shining spirits? Their sorrow is already being transmuted to gold, given in love and human joy to others of their beloved group. The pain of their handicapped existence is fleeting. The soul's benefits endure forever.

Such assignments are the group's work. There is work at every level of the ascending spiritual kingdoms. Work and love form the ground of happiness in both human life and universal life. For a long time, in our world, work and love are separate. They are combined, however, in the creative, self-actualized human being, who is achieving oneness within. The combination of work and love becomes a further satisfaction of the craving for union.

Looking about, we can see the ways in which that craving finds satisfaction, imitation or genuine. The great completions that lie ahead for us all are the twin union and the group union. Genuine items, they are blueprints for our society's imitations: romance and conformity. The twin union is constantly and brightly foreshadowed in films and romance novels. The public hungrily gobbles up the scripts, then plays out the drama over and over in life.

Romantic love is a necessity. It is the rehearsal for the real. In time the characters become more mature, better able to distinguish between reality and dream. Through these lessons of love, the distance to the twin slowly closes.

Conformity, union's poor relation, expresses the great need of the soul to be close to other like souls. To have the same car as others, the same house, the same clothes—above all, the same ideas—is to be no longer separate. It evokes, at oceanic depths, the sense of being embraced and held, as the soul was held in embryonic closeness so long ago in the great womb of the undifferentiated group.

This, too, is playing out a genuine need. But there is a fatal flaw in the scenario: conformity prohibits the growth of the individual. And only developed individuals can genuinely unite, coming together in love founded on admiration, respect, and the creative joy of making new discoveries in each other day by day. These mutual discoveries spark the continual growth that is the true measure of soul bonding.

Conformity is particularly compelling in adolescence. That the drive to conform keeps its grip on most throughout their lives indicates that our earthly society is still in the adolescent phase of evolution. There is much dark-force encouragement in the conforming society, as evidenced by its greed for material possessions, its jealousies, competitiveness, and scorn for spiritual values.

But all this is changing. The new wave continues sweeping in, despite opposition. It is apparent on a grand scale in times of world catastrophe; there is a rushing together, even of old enemies, to unite in common cause and aid the stricken. At the individual level, people are drawing together for self-improvement and discovery through group therapy. They come to it from self-need, but in the process, boundaries between themselves and others are dissolved. A psychiatrist reports the story of Gail, a woman in one of his therapy groups. She decided at one point that she wanted to leave the group for another, where she might be better understood. She wanted a deeper experience, she said. The psychiatrist was willing to let her go:

> I then got the idea that what Gail was really saying was, "I want to get into my deeper feelings so that I can be fully understood."

I said to her, "I think you are bringing out your deeper feeling, the feeling that you'll never be understood—as you were never understood in your childhood." She had been raised by elderly parents who were extremely distant. "I think *this* is the deep feeling," I went on. "This is the theme of your life." She replied: "But you can never be completely understood." Something made me say, "Yes you can." I was thinking, of course, in spiritual terms.

Gail went on to say, "But rather than not be completely understood I'd rather not try, I'd rather stay away." I considered, then told her, "I could understand that, but by doing so you keep complete understanding away: you keep yourself at a distance and build up loneliness. Indeed you've had one of the most lonely times I have ever heard of, from the day you were born."

Soon I detected a slight shade of sadness in Gail's eyes and was moved to say, "There it is. You're feeling sad now, are you not?" She admitted that she was. I said, "Let it come, let it come." And the tears began to roll. Another woman patient reached out and touched her, held her hand, and I moved over and held her other hand, quietly whispering, "Keep it coming, keep it coming." And so she cried, this woman who normally was jacketed in defensive armor. The tears continued to flow—I wiped her cheek with a tissue—and so it went quietly for a time. Finally she took a deep breath and said she was better.

I said to her, "This is part of being completely understood. And how much better you look! How beautiful you look!" For she did; she was transfused. I looked around at the group and saw that everybody's face was aglow—with happiness, a kind of joyous sympathy, and love. I told her to look around at these faces. "See what you've done for them as well as yourself." I then spoke about this love in the room as being spiritual and true. "*This* is spirituality. This is what the world can be like. This joy and this love is what comes forth after the false skin that society and conditioning put upon us is melted."

The members of society who have begun to acquire individuality will rise above the conforming mass and assert their selfhood. They will turn from the artificial security of the uncaring group and move toward their soul group and their twin, braving the loneliness of the path to self-discovery. They had been trying to find the other while the self was still unformed.

The growth of self is central—but only for a time. Many people insist that no other is needed, that the way to salvation lies wholly within oneself. But finally we all must ask, "What is my selfhood for?" The soul knows the answer. "It is for other."

Our self-development has one purpose: that we may learn to love. Were it not for the love of others, we would be closed in with ourselves forever. Some would say, "As I find myself, I can love others." Yes, but love as we know it is partial. It travels on a two-way track, from me to you and from you to me. We remain separated. There is a space between us. That is where the dark forces stand always ready to invade. It is there that so many lovers are cut down, and their love deflected onto the long slide toward hate.

The wholeness of love occurs only when I *become* you and you become me. That is supreme empathic bonding. That is soul love and the way of complete understanding. It comes in the union with the other of our self, the twin soul. Our growth in love is all for this. Our twin union is all for the broader love of the soul family.

In well-conducted group therapy, the group members emerge with feelings of family union, a love for each of the others. Thus, group therapy prepares one for the expansive love of the soul family. Let us look at the experience of Bill, a man strongly inhibited in the recognition of his emotions and most especially in his fear of abandonment. His group therapist took strenuous action. He asked the others in the group to leave Bill in the room by himself. As the group began to exit, three members decided they could not go along with this maneuver. They remained with Bill, rather than "abandon" him.

Afterward, when the event was reviewed, Bill revealed (with much emotion) that it had made a major impact upon him. For him it was a turning point. He realized that these three people had no obligation to him; they were, in fact, virtual strangers. Yet for the sake of love alone, from their caring, they stayed with him and defied the authority of the therapist. Bill was so impressed that he dropped his overt caution and decided that people were perhaps trustworthy, after all. He expressed his enormous gratitude to the three others. The therapist and the rest of the group added their agreement, giving support, speaking of their own gratitude. Thereupon the group cohesiveness and group energy was confirmed and advanced.

This may or may not be an example of group soulship. It does not prove that these people descended together from a common soul. Perhaps they did; or perhaps they were guided to come together in this particular instance of group therapy. It does illustrate group energy and group love emergent. Certainly the members were ready to knit and to support and to express sublimated love for each other.

Why is it important that we know the laws, the plan, and the pattern of reuniting? Because if evolution were just left to itself to carry us along, it would take forever! It is better to spend our eternity in a state of bliss and arrive at that state as quickly as we can. The Universe has given us the schemata for direct progress. It amounts to joining the dots. The first two are the twin souls, then the line moves through the groups. The line that joins each of us to our twin is traced by both of us at once; the progress of one is matched by the other. Emotions in the heart of one enter the heart that beats in resonance with it half a universe away or just around the corner. To feel hopeless, to despair of finding love, holds us apart. As we learn and know that the other exists, hope flows between us and draws us closer. The connection is constant and unbroken. None of us is in isolation. The essential interplay between two is a law of Nature and is reflected in physics.

The Nobel-prize-winning physicist Richard Feynman discovered that an electron that emits a light particle (photon) must interact with another electron that absorbs the particle. Further studies in time direction led to the astonishing conclusion that emission of a light particle millions of years ago by an electron in a distant star was triggered by the advance wave from another electron here at the present time. This may be useful to remember as we try to contemplate the cosmic maneuvering of twin souls toward one another.

There is another problem with entrusting our course wholly to evolution. The life-flow has two directions, upward and downward. Nature, abhoring a vacuum, allows no drift. If not actively working our way up, we fall back. Normally we can make up the loss, for the loss is part of our learning. But what of those souls who allow themselves to be pulled down for their entire lifetimes by the powers of Darkness? Where today are the souls of Adolf Hitler and other villains in history?

Consider the gangster, defying the laws of man and ignorant of the higher, creating for himself future lives of crushing karmic debt. Will he be able to pay without a gun in his back? Strength of soul is required for such payment, and he has not been working at that kind of strength. And so his descent, and that of others like him, will continue, ever perpetuating itself. There will be a group soul, but distant, not close, for the closeness has never been established.

Universal forces of many kinds will attempt to reverse the direction of the souls who are falling; but the choice at each stage remains theirs. What will become of them? Shall they not ever be taken back into God, the Source of all extending and returning life?

Yes, each will return, but as smoke from a fire, the immolation of what might have been a masterpiece. In direct contrast to those who return in full consciousness to the heights of unity, those in the depths gradually separate once more into isolated units. Consciousness fades and flickers out. As individuals they cease to exist. This is the ultimate separation, the reabsorption into the original Creative Substance, to await a new beginning and new soul-identity in the next cycle of creation.

Anna Kingsford, a leading member of the British Theosophical Society in the early 1900s gave us the following vision, which helps to explain:

> I see a lake, vast and deep and bright. A lake or sea; it has no
> borders that I can perceive. Its waters are so clear that I could see

the pebbles shining at the bottom if it had one. It is overspread by a flood of nebulous light, evenly diffused in all parts; and now, as I look, the light has become concentrated into flowers, and between them are spaces of darkness caused by the withdrawal of the light into the flowers. It is a vast floating garden of flowers, and in the midst of the garden is a tree. The tree spreads out its arms everywhere. The garden is creation, the tree is God. And the tree seems in some way to be the flowers, and the flowers belong to the tree. The material of the tree is not matter: it is the substance of matter, the divinity underlying it. God is not light, but that of which light itself is the manifestation. God willed it to be. Light is the result of God's will. God said, "Let light be;" and it was. Matter is the intensification of Idea. All things are made of God's thought. God is Spirit, and the substance of things. I see two forces ever in operation: they are the centrifugal and the centripetal. And they are one: yes, one and the same, for I see the force rebound back to God. Creation is ever being projected from God as from a luminous centre; it is always being drawn back again also. Some parts refuse to return; they go into outer space; they are lost. Let me see—can it be that they pass beyond the sphere of the Divine Attraction? Yes; I see that it is so, and oh! they are lost. The Spirit is withdrawn; it is as if it were sucked out of them, and they wander away into darkness, and expend themselves. The rest, who approach God, develop, the Spirit in them becoming more and more like God. God is the richer for them. They continue to exist. They return, but do not become lost in God.

It is extremely important that we know the game is real. The Plan for the reuniting of souls at the source is for all to return in the precise order of their fall-out. "God ever geometrizes," said da Vinci. But the Plan carries within it the seed of its own disruption: the free will of the individual. By their own choice, some souls will lag behind, at risk of being pulled out of position. The Separatists, or Brothers of the Shadow as they are termed in Theosophy, never slacken in their efforts to drag back into primal chaos those who, like Lucifer, will not serve.

Security comes with the group union. Service and devotion are the rule among the souls within it. If one slips, rescue is nearby. Every group is composed of twin souls, perhaps joined, perhaps drawing together within it. We might wonder whether safety is assured as the twins reunite. Not necessarily. The point of union may be the time of greatest danger.

Picture a pyramid, one side in sunlight, the opposite in shadow. We have been scaling the pyramid as the first great phase of our evolutionary climb. We approach the pinnacle where the twin is to be found, and just there at the tip, where we are closest to the light, we are also closest to the dark. It is then that the concentrated dark strike may come, always unexpected and always heavily disguised.

If one of the twins is tipped downward, through obsession or delusion, what happens to the other? The other will come to the rescue, aided by all the force of the group. The deluded person, for instance, may have become a channeler or an astral entity, posing as a "great teacher from the other side," as so many of them do. The channeler has perhaps lost all sense of reality and is drugged with power, the most dangerous trip of all. Perhaps the group members become the teacher's disciples, forming a protective circle all around and channeling in turn through their own intuition the genuine light that might one day break through.

But if in the end the evil grip is too strong, the one twin will be pulled down with the other. This is the only true tragedy. Greek drama chills us with the death of kings, but those are as nothing compared with the death of a soul.

The fall is long. The rescue attempts continue into the depths, as dramatically evoked in this excerpt from *The Continuing City,* a novel about reincarnation:

First is a riddle: How do Departure and Return divide into three?

It is as simple as everything else. Departure has just one direction; but there are two ways of Return.

Oh thou soul, endowed with the dignity of choice, which will you take, the race toward life or drift toward death? Will you labor to scale the pinnacle of Selfhood, alone leading to union and bliss, or by way of descent, through dimming consciousness and the unravelling of Self, re-enter the Unformed and await a new Creation?

Here—oh look quickly before it hides behind one of its thousand masks—here it lies, coiled at the centre of every fear known to humankind—the Original Fear: loss of being. Ages-old, primeval fear, fear of the fall from *I am* to *I am not*, formless recall from before the long breath of Creation, from the very deeps of the Mind of God, where dissolution and reabsorption are purged of their agony and the terror passes into the Great Memory.

To be obliterated, extinguished, waters closing over where once was I, individual, unique among others. And is it with the spiritual death as with the small human dying, that the whole life repeats before the eye in its moment of closing?

Think of it! The I, perceived all at once, its infinitude finally encapsuled, too late revealed. I! formed from a thousand forms, made from billions of years, millions of births and deaths, composed more of minutes and seconds than of years, for I cannot exult in a year but can feel an instant expand me to the limits of joy, a limit always widening toward the limitless. I, born and cherished of families uncounted, perhaps exalted by multitudes, revered in the trappings of royalty, no doubt burned at stakes and hanged from ancient trees ... and no scrap of it without purpose and gain. I of so many talents! My fingers hold memories of stringed instruments, sculptors' clay, soft hair of my thousands of children. I have spoken with the tongues of all countries, lived, bled and died in the skin of all races, inhabited cities now buried deep under the earth, their life still vibrant within the Collective Mind.

And always, in all times and all places, I have loved. I have followed, hand over hand, the invisible thread that runs through the centre of all and which, if it were to be snapped, would cause the whole of Creation to spill into the Void.

I am fed by the Universe and feed it also, for all that I gain by my labors is given into the whole; and all others' advances advance me, enmeshed in the web of the great purposeful Life.

But if I move out of position, disturbing the exquisite balance which holds me in perfect relation to all? There will be an immense shift in the whole as aid rushes to me. But I am the mover and chooser, and respect will be shown for my will. I may refuse the aid: I am allowed. I may fall. I may vacate my place: none will refuse me. Perhaps I spin, free-falling and laughing at the serious God, planning to stop myself when I please.

And long ages after, deep in my fall, when I am helpless and will-less, even though all Life be held out to stay me, I still must make the saving grasp—and find I cannot.

Now to the mourning of God is added the necessity of mending the fabric of the once-perfect Work. Such a small tear—might not it be patched? ... or the space pulled together by a mere closing-in of the nearest souls in the hierarchy of rejoining?

No: the great mathematical scheme of Departure and Return does not permit a simple adjustment. Where the smallest part is affected, the largest is equally affected. In torment and groaning labor the entire created universe reassembles itself, from the far firmaments to the tiny unopened eye of the embryo fieldmouse. Oh, had I known my immense significance!

CHAPTER FIVE

TWIN SOULS
IN LITERATURE
AND HISTORY

S HAKESPEARE'S *Romeo and Juliet* deals with the meeting of twin souls." So writes the Master Omraam Aivanhov. "But this meeting brings about their deaths, because the conditions of our existence do not permit the realization of such a perfect love, such absolute love."

The immortal quality of the love between two people whose souls are twin to each other has provided the inspiration for all the world's great love stories: *Romeo and Juliet, Tristan and Isolde, Wuthering Heights.* It is also the foundation of the famous true-life loves: Dante and Beatrice, Petrarch and Laura, Abelard and Heloise.

Wuthering Heights, an imperishable love story, was first considered such a risk by its publishers that Emily Brontë had to defray the cost of publication until a sufficient number of copies had been sold. Set on the Yorkshire moors of nineteenth-century England, it tells of the fierce, tormented love between Cathy and Heathcliff, who become lost in each other, each possessing the other's spirit equally with their own. When Cathy dies in childbirth, Heathcliff, mad with grief, cries out, "I cannot live without my soul!"

Most of these stories, the fictional and the real, culminate in tragedy. Aivanhov is right in saying that the conditions of our existence have not permitted the realization of such absolute love. But the conditions of existence have been changing. The very purpose of human advancement is the possibility and realization of higher states of love. We can trace this advance in the examples of fulfilled love that history provides. In the following pages we will examine a few of these, marriages between lovers rich in accomplishment and service to the world, the marriages ideally happy and marked with the distinguishing signs of twin-soulship. This is most notable with the poets Elizabeth and Robert Browning, and the scientists Marie and Pierre Curie.

Such heroic twin-soul lovers provide inspiration to us all. They are models for everyone, for the future near and distant, a future that is racing toward us. Given the signs close at hand, we may be certain that twin souls are meeting all across the world and generating the love that will transform this earth.

Biographies written about the Brownings and the Curies describe marriages that were rare and flawless, the respective artistic and scientific works conducted in the steady light of an enduring love. There was no competition, no friction between husband and wife, for the partners were of equal caliber and identical power of achievement.

Elizabeth Barrett and Robert Browning are twin giants in English poetry. They came together in mid-nineteenth-century London, when Robert wrote to Elizabeth in praise of her work. Elizabeth was already renowned as a poet. It would be twenty years before Robert would achieve comparable fame. She, six years older, perceived the products of his struggling youth as superior to hers; all their lives each would insist that the other was the greater poet.

Their correspondence became a major contribution to literature, as well. It was prodigious, 573 letters extant, one of the longest, fullest, most self-contained correspondences in English literary history. The reason for their incessant letter-writing to each other was that Elizabeth was a virtual prisoner in her home on Wimpole Street. Under the domination of a possessive father, she was made invalid and confined to her couch, forbidden the companionship of any but her sisters. Of the senior Barrett she wrote: "He would sooner see me dead at his feet than belong to another." She was cured by Robert's love and in September, 1846, spirited away to Italy, where they made their home. Following the elopement, her father returned all her letters unopened and did not permit her name to be mentioned again in his house.

The courtship was conducted through the letters and brief visits by Robert, with the complicity of her sisters. We can thank the circumstances now, for the letters have provided us with an unimpeachable record of twin-soul love and relatedness. The gender identity of the two poets stands out clearly, constantly reiterated in statements made by and about them. Describing Robert in a letter, Elizabeth wrote: "The intellect is little in comparison to all the rest—to the womanly tenderness, the inexhaustible goodness, the high and noble aspiration of every hour. Temper, spirits, manners—there is not a flaw anywhere."

To Robert himself, she wrote: "You are 'masculine' to the height—and I, as a woman, have studied some of your gestures of language and intonation wistfully, as a thing beyond me far! and the more admirable for being beyond."

We see Browning as an embodiment of the evolved masculine soul, his "womanly tenderness" in balance and blend with his strengths. A perceptive biographer, Osbert Burdett, gives a capsule description of Browning's masculinity when he says of the letters, "Except in their sincerity his are the exact opposite of hers. Grace, vividness, charm are not the qualities of his side of their correspondence. His letters are rugged and rough and tender and patient and considerate and strong."

Of Elizabeth, Burdett writes: "In the best of her work, as in her life, she was his complement, but unlike some women of genius she was wholly feminine ... One is inclined to say that with any other husband she would have collapsed. The love that never fails was his ... The dream that is so often indulged, so rarely realized, was fulfilled for this pair, and it is idle to attempt to communicate their possession. It makes us realize afresh how exceptional is such mutual affection, how rare a marriage like this."

The biographer with no conscious knowledge of the twinship of souls is often its best exponent, for he speaks without bias. Here Burdett gives a fairly complete description of twin souls:

> Both poets make us realize the beauty of character, and it may be said of her [Barrett], as she said of Browning, that the least important part about him was his genius. When therefore a poet appears whose character rings as true as his genius, we have an unusual opportunity. We are unexpectedly forced to set two beauties side by side, and can judge them without prejudice. In Browning we take the genius for granted and can look at the man, and the man, whose imagination has already won our homage, proves a revelation. For once, there are no buts on either side, and the effect is to make us see high character poetically. It is as if the poet had opened a new loveliness to our eyes, as if there were a new possibility of beauty for us in human relations. Art is so often our consolation that it is refreshing to be able to regard it as the grace of a life already noble. Judging by its own measure the world has called Browning conventional. *The truth is that he was whole.*
>
> As a man and artist he was masculine to the core. There was no want of balance in his genius. His life and work prove that the supposed alliance of great wits and madness is not essential … He had an immense capacity for affection, and this capacity was equalled by his wife. The only circumstance that hit him to the heart was her death when both were middle-aged. In gifts, in love, in fortune, Fate played into his hands. If this world had been his main concern he would have had almost everything, but he looked beyond it, and the great question of what lay beyond was bound up for him with the loss of his wife. Human love had meant everything to him. Consequently, when death took her away, the centre of his being hung in the balance, and his inner life was ruled by hope and fear for nearly thirty years after she died.
>
> It is clear that only a remarkable woman could have held and

maintained this central place in a life of such splendid energy. She was as nearly his religion as one person can be to another.... They possessed the experience (of love) as rare in fact as it is in fiction. It survived every test. He was thirty-three before he became engaged; he was a husband for fifteen years; he lived for twenty-eight years a widower. There was only one love in his life, and only one in hers. Despite all the conventions to the contrary, this is a strange and wonderful thing. Among love stories it is a fairy tale, and it is true.

That two human beings capable of this experience should realize it together is exceptional; that both should be poets is doubly strange. In their life and in their work they were the complementary opposites of one another. She was feminine to the marrow, and only became a complete poet when she put her woman's response to his love into verse. The very circumstances of her early years were the feminine counterpart of his. He had all the world before him, masculine energy and a free life. She had ill-health, a sofa and her books only. In her family she was a prisoner living at the whim of her autocratic father, whereas he was happy and untrammelled in his home. Both were scholars and widely read, but, unlike him, she preserved the innocence of childlike faith quite untroubled by her reading or the scepticism of her time....

Perhaps we may sum up their relation by saying that she was that which Shelley had promised, but failed to remain: a lyric poet of love "showing the correspondency of the natural to the spiritual," a human being "tender and sincere," who, through her capacity for love, radiated something of divine power and influence.

If the Brownings radiated to the world a divine power through their art, the gift was paralleled in science by Pierre Curie, the French physicist, and his Polish wife, Marie. The Curies were married in Paris in 1895, and in 1903 jointly received a Nobel prize for their work with radioactivity. Although the scientific establishment initially opposed them, their discovery of radium proved epochal and finally forced a reconsideration of the foundation of physics and chemistry.

They were a true example of twin-soul love, with their contribution to the world on the one hand, and the immense happiness of their personal lives on the other. The Curies' marriage was as close to perfection as this earth allows. Of Pierre, Marie wrote: "I have the best husband one could dream of; I could never have imagined finding one like him. He is a true gift of heaven, and the more we live together the more we love each other."

Their life together was shattered, suddenly and tragically, on April 19, 1906, when Pierre was run over by a dray on the rue Dauphine in Paris and instantly killed. Marie continued her life in science and the care of their two daughters, the older of whom would later win a Nobel prize of her own. In 1909 Marie was named to her husband's chair in physics at the Sorbonne, and in 1911 she was awarded a Nobel prize for her isolation of radium and her studies in its chemistry. She was the only person ever to have been awarded the Nobel prize in both physics and chemistry.

The yin intuitive faculty played a large part in the Curies' destiny, for at first Marie only guessed at the possible existence of the new element, radium. To prove its existence she used her highly evolved yang strength and determination in a physical and mental labor that would have exhausted anyone else, men included. The radium had to be extracted in an interminably slow process from pitchblende, one ton of pitchblende yielding a mere one-tenth gram of radium chloride in the early experiments. Pierre aided her in this work in a spirit of protectiveness and support, which is wholly masculine. At the same time he showed the yin qualities that enabled him to share the management of a home and children, while leading a life dedicated to scientific pursuit.

Their younger daughter, Eve, in her biography, *Madame Curie,* gives us the distinctive twin-soul description:

The two souls, like the two brains, were of equal quality. They formed one of the finest bonds that ever united man and woman. Two hearts beat together, two bodies were united, and two minds of genius learned to think together. Marie could have married no other than this great physicist, than this wise and noble man; Pierre could have married no woman other than the fair, tender Polish girl, who could be childish or transcendent within the same few moments; for she was a friend and a wife, a lover and a scientist.

After Pierre's death, there was no question of remarriage. There was never any other man in Marie's life, before or after her union with Pierre, nor any other woman in his. The same was true of the Brownings. It is safe to suppose that these four souls came into incarnation prepared for the twin union. They were ready for absolute fidelity. Readiness comes when sexual trial and learning have been completed—possibly in previous lives.

We might even imagine, if only for study purposes, the Brownings and the Curies occupying adjacent positions in the group soul. The two couples would then have been next-of-twin. Next-of-twin couples will most probably complement each other in mentality, each pair representing one of the two great streams of human endeavor, art or science. Creative scientific thinkers such as Gary Zukav have recognized these differences. In *The Dancing Wu Li Masters* he writes: "Generally speaking, people can be grouped into two categories of intellectual preference." The first group he refers to as possessing a scientific mental set, and the second, an artistic mental set.

The examples of twin souls that we know of indicate that twins are of the same mental set. In reality they are one soul, and therefore engaged in complementary aspects of the same work. The work is either artistic, as with the Brownings, or scientific, as with the Curies. They then require the balancing complement of their next-of-twin, the foursome making a more complete whole.

Some educators are discovering that the two types of mentality—artistic and scientific—are indicated in children, though they are of course mingled. The suggestion has been put forward that the two types need different methods of teaching. With increased recognition of spiritual endowments, this is a definite possibility.

Art and science could be thought of respectively as the yin and yang of mentalities, each with the contra-mentality present, in the same pattern as the opposite genders. As the highly evolved man is developed also in his feminine aspects, the highly evolved scientist is likely to be a burgeoning artist. Einstein played the violin; Churchill, that great political scientist, became a painter of note. Perhaps the most outstanding example of artistic mentality with a scientific interior is Leonardo da Vinci, who long before their invention, sketched the submarine, the airplane, and, alas, the machine gun. Da Vinci showed that at a very high stage of evolvement the complementary mental streams can become virtually equal. It is the same with the opposite genders in the hermaphrodite, that is in the ultimate stage of spiritual union. In neither case do they melt into the other, but retain their distinction within the whole.

Reuniting twin souls will be found to be gifted in science or art or a mutation of these. They will benefit next from meeting their next-of-twins, the opposite mental types, the pair who separated out with them in the last stages of the descent. If they meet with their next-of-twins in this life, a new balance is achieved, with a further generating of love. It is a higher completion. The completions will continue in unending sequence all the way up to the final union of all.

The process may sound too ideal, or as some would say, too good to be true. Yet, when faced with the dark-force activity in the world, the same people would have to say that that activity is too *bad* to be true.

The too-good and the too-bad modify each other, as we have seen. The dark force has its constructive uses, and the bright picture of twin love is never without its shadings. Despite all opposition, the Brownings and the Curies were able to fight through and realize the promise of their lives and their work. So rarely does history portray this fulfillment of great love and high achievement that we are left to wonder how many twin souls have been intercepted at the point of union, and how much noble work intended for the world has failed to be born.

One of the most vivid twin-soul tragedies is the story of the twelfth-century lovers Abelard and Heloise. Peter Abelard was a French philosopher and theologian, a brilliant teacher and dialectician, as well as a leading figure in medieval scholasticism. Heloise was the niece of a canon. Her love affair with Abelard resulted in the birth of a child and a subsequent secret marriage. Heloise's uncle took revenge on Abelard by having him kidnapped and emasculated.

Following this cruel punishment, Abelard entered religious life. Long afterward he could write of it to Heloise as an act of God's mercy that rid him of the torments of the flesh. But what he vividly recalls in his *Historia* is the pain and horror, his feelings of humiliation and disgust at being a eunuch, the unclean beast of Jewish law. He admits that "it was shame and confusion in my remorse and misery rather than any devout wish for conversion which brought me to seek shelter in a monastery cloister."

Heloise, following the pattern of their shared destiny, joined the Benedictine order of nuns, and would later become Mother Superior of the convent of the Paraclete, established by Abelard. It is believed that their famous letters were exchanged at this period.

Their love has cast a light across the centuries, providing material for works of tragic literature even to this day. The twin pattern is evident: their intellectual statures were on an equal plane; their gifts and life works were the same. Their complementary genders were in balance. In *The Immortal Lovers*, Marjorie Worthington writes: "Heloise, for all her intellectual attainment and for all her strength of character, never lets us forget how utterly feminine she was."

Their service to the dark and superstitious world of their time did not come without tremendous cost. The pain of their forced separation was a wound that had no healing in their lifetime. Heloise's pain is poured out in her letters:

The pleasures of lovers which we shared ... can scarcely be banished from my thoughts. Wherever I turn they are always there before my eyes, bringing with them awakened longings and fantasies which will not even let me sleep. Even during the celebration of the Mass, where our prayers should be purer, lewd visions of those pleasures take such a hold upon my unhappy soul that my thoughts are on their wantonness instead of on prayers. I should be groaning over the sins I have committed, but I can only sigh for what I have lost. Everything we did and also the times and places are stamped on my heart along with your image, so that I live through it all again with you. Even in sleep I know no respite. Sometimes my thoughts are betrayed in a movement of my body, or they break out in an unguarded word. In my utter wretchedness, that cry from a suffering soul could well be mine: "Miserable creature that I am, who is there to rescue me out of the body doomed to this death?" Would that in truth I could go on: "The grace of God through Jesus Christ our Lord." This grace, my dearest, came upon you unsought—a single wound of the body by freeing you from these torments has healed many wounds in your soul…. But for me, youth and passion and experience of pleasures which were so delightful intensify the torments of the flesh and longings of desire, and the assault is the more overwhelming as the nature they attack is the weaker. Men call me chaste; they do not know the hypocrite I am. They consider purity of the flesh a virtue, though virtue belongs not to the body but to the soul.

Abelard responds to her from his intellect and his place of priestly detachment:

When I am suffering in despair of my life, would it be fitting for you to be joyous? Would you want to be partners only in joy, not grief, to join in rejoicing without weeping with those who weep? … I come at last to your old perpetual complaint, in which you presume to blame God for the manner of our entry into religion instead of wishing to glorify him as you justly should… Remember what you have said, recall what you have written, namely that in the manner of our conversion, when God seems to have been more my adversary, he had clearly shown himself kinder.... You should not grieve because you are the cause of so great a good, for which you must not doubt you were specially created by God.... See then, my beloved, see how with the drag-nets of his mercy the Lord has fished us up from the depths of this dangerous sea, although we were unwilling, so that each of us may justly break out in that cry: "The Lord takes thought for me." ... Comfort by our example any unrighteous who despair of God's goodness, so that all may know what may be done for those who ask with prayer, when such benefits are granted sinners even against their will.

There can be little doubt that the tragedy of these lovers was the work of separative forces, though ultimately, as always, the results were to serve a higher purpose. Part of that purpose was to bring their love story to the forefront of human legend.

The dark powers that struck Abelard and Heloise early in their union succeeded with Clara and Robert Schumann at a later stage. The Schumanns were another pair with all the signs of twin-soul love. The great nineteenth-century German composer was an estab-lished concert pianist when he met the nine-year-old Clara. She was already a virtuoso at the keyboard and destined to become the most celebrated woman pianist of her time. They fell in love gradually, as Schumann watched a delightful, gifted child blossom into a beau-tiful young woman. He proposed marriage when she was fifteen.

Here the opposition took the same form as with Elizabeth Barrett: a consuming and possessive father. Clara's father, the noted piano teacher Friedrich Wieck, refused to allow the marriage and tried in every way to stop the love developing between his daughter and Robert Schumann. Three years later the lovers went to court to force his consent to their marriage.

The marriage took place in 1840, whereupon Schumann literally burst into song. The year 1840 has been called "the song year," with one masterpiece following another. The year 1841 was "the symphony year," and 1842 the "chamber music" year. It was as though Schumann knew that something evil was pursuing him—as it was. Long haunted by fear of insanity, he had made suicide attempts earlier in his life. The years of happiness with Clara were short. By the late 1840s Schumann was suffering increasingly from bouts with mental illness. Long periods of depression now began to affect his work. Many lofty conceptions for works were never fulfilled, although he wrote several masterpieces, among them the Piano Concerto in A minor. Most of his other compositions of that period were the product of a sick mind. The symptoms of severe illness became more frequent, and in 1854 he was committed to an asylum. Fifteen years after joining his life with Clara's he was hopelessly insane. This is a dramatic example of the dark-force influence, and may one day be proved to be present in all cases of mental illness.

It is not coincidental that Johannes Brahms had become a close friend of the Schumanns' and had fallen in love with Clara. These three undoubtedly belonged to the great musical group soul incarnating at that period. Group-soul love has very specific purposes, in this instance the devoted friendship and consolation Brahms was able to provide Clara in the absence of her twin. Brahms loved her in substitute for his own twin soul.

But where was his twin? Where was Beethoven's? Why do some advanced souls come into incarnation to meet their twin, while most do not? We can only surmise. Perhaps a great many do incarnate with the meeting in their life-plan, but are kept from it by the forces of separation. Or it may be that the twin has been joined in a former life on earth or in spirit dimensions. The inspiration from the unseen half of the soul may have contributed to the great musical works of Beethoven and Brahms. Perhaps the circumstances were chosen, for singleness of focus on their life task. The human loneliness, contrasted with the spiritual union once known, could account for the personal misery that these artists endured throughout most of their lives.

If Schumann's soul, before incarnation, chose rather to have his twin at his side in mortal life, he paid a high price for it. Perhaps the powers of Darkness can gain greater leverage with both twins on the physical level—always depending, of course, on the karmic record of each individual.

As for Beethoven, historians have never been able to clearly identify the woman whom he mentioned in a letter as "my immortal beloved." The description did not seem to fit any of the women the composer knew and disastrously loved. Could the "immortal beloved" have referred to the twin, invisible at his side, his soul remembering while he, the man, did not?

In contrast to the cases just cited, are unions that seem impervious to obstruction. One of the happiest that history records is that of John Stuart Mill and Harriet Taylor. These two were brought together in London, England, at the end of the 1820s. Mill, recognized in his life as the foremost social thinker of his time, shaped the bedrock of political science, with influences extending throughout the democratic institutions that we enjoy today. Harriet was a young woman of brilliant mentality, unhappily married to a man who was kindly but very much her intellectual inferior. Her misery at the empty companionship and the stultification of her faculties finally sent her to seek the counsel of her Unitarian minister, William Johnson Fox. This remarkable man took seriously her desire for equal companionship. Instead of preaching Victorian principles, he offered to introduce her to John Stuart Mill.

Mill was twenty-four, a year older than Harriet, and had already achieved renown with his essay, *The Spirit of the Age.* His need was as great as Harriet's, though in the direction of the emotions. He had a mind that had been honed into a fine machine capable of radical thought and practical reform; but in the way of machines, his mind had broken down. He had sunk deep into depression. He wrote:

> It occurred to me to put the question directly to myself: "Suppose that all your objects in life were realized; that all the changes in institutions and opinions which you are looking forward to, could be completely effected at this very instant: would this be a great joy and happiness to you?" And an irrepressible self-consciousness distinctly answered, "No!" At this

my heart sank within me: the whole foundation on which my life was constructed fell down. All my happiness was to have been found in the continual pursuit of this end. The end had ceased to charm, and how could there ever again be any interest in the means? I seemed to have nothing left to live for.

He was to discover, in finding Harriet Taylor, that he had *everything* to live for. He was imbalanced in the direction of thought; she balanced him with her own feeling nature. He later wrote:

I had always wished for a friend whom I could admire wholly, without reservation and restriction, and now I had found one. To render this possible it was necessary that the object of my admiration should be of a type different from my own; should be a character preeminently of feeling, combined however, as I had not in any other instance known it to be, with a vigorous and bold speculative intellect.

Very soon after their meeting, he and Harriet were deeply involved, writing essays together, seeing each other daily and exchanging fervent letters. This was the companionship that she, too, had longed for. As Mill needed emotional sustenance, she had hungered for the nourishment of a mind akin to her own, of which there were not many in England. The unusual way in which her appeal to her minister was answered allows us to see the inevitability of the twin-soul meeting when the right time has arrived.

Almost at a stroke, they made the leap to the gender balance that defines the twin souls. Their intellects matched, and their two dispositions complemented each other. Where he was careful, she was daring; where he was detached and balanced, she was partial and intuitive. Mill felt as though another world had been opened to him. This was what he had missed in his arid intellectualism: beauty and passion. He had always pursued the good and the true, but without drawing upon his deepest vitality. He admired people who were spontaneous and enthusiastic, who believed what they believed with emotion, not always from pure logic. For this reason he adored the company of Harriet Taylor and never ceased to think of her as a better human being than himself.

Harriet, for her part, coped valiantly with the love triangle. She candidly faced her husband with her feelings for Mill. John Taylor asked her to renounce sight of Mill and she agreed. Then she found that she could not do without her friend, and her husband could not bear to see her so unhappy. Gradually Mill was sanctioned in the role of platonic lover and was at the Taylors' house every night of the week.

In their consideration of whether Harriet should leave her husband and live with Mill, they brought to the drama of their own lives all the scrupulous consideration they devoted to the theoretical problems of justice in society. They determined that nothing could justify so great an injury to John Taylor except the certain knowledge that they would be insupportably unhappy if they did not live together. Their personal ethics demanded that they ask the question: How is the greatest quantity of unhappiness to be avoided? These two people of strong will and reason and undoubted passions decided at last that the least unhappiness would result from Harriet's staying with Taylor, provided she could continue to enjoy the company of Mill.

In the more than twenty years that passed before they were free to marry they produced all the major works that bear Mill's name but that he declared were joint productions. He wrote: "Not only during the years of our married life, but during many years of confidential friendship which preceded it, all my published writings are as much my wife's work as mine." They include: *Principles of Political Economy, On Liberty, The Autobiography, The Subjection of Women,* and the numerous essays on religion. Some of these works were published only after Harriet's death, a mere seven years after their marriage, but they had been discussed, drafted, planned, and in some cases dictated by her, long before their actual release. His belief was that when two people together probe every subject of interest, when they hold all thoughts and speculations in common, whatever writings may result are joint products. The one who has contributed the least to composition may have contributed the most to thought. It is of little consequence which of them holds the pen.

On the death of John Taylor, they scarcely felt the need to marry, so closely were their minds and souls already wedded. They submitted to a marriage ceremony only so that they could live under the same roof and not waste the time of traveling to each other daily. They took a secluded house and were supremely happy, discussing everything, sharing everything, dedicated to their writing. Neither had any interest in the artificial pleasures of society, for they found each other absolutely fascinating, and the fascination never dimmed.

There is in twin souls a certain obedience to each other, not unlike the mystic's obedience to God. While standing strong within themselves, they are quick to defer to each other, from a deeply felt sense that the other is in a way their best self. This sense was very strongly marked in John Stuart Mill, more so than in Harriet. He wrote at her direction, saying once, typically, "I want my angel to tell me what should be the next essay written. I have done all I can for the subject she last gave me." And she replied, "About the essays, dear, would not religion, the Utility of Religion, be one of the subjects you have most to say on?"

His mind was one of the amazing phenomena of the age; his skull is reported to have contained the largest brain size known to science, yet the feeling part of himself, required to mobilize thought, dwelt in Harriet. He wrote to her: "What would be the use of my outliving you! I could write nothing worth keeping alive except with your prompting."

Some biographers believe that the Mills' relationship may have been nonsexual. Physical love may have been ruined for Harriet after having to endure unwanted sexual intercourse with her husband before meeting John Stuart, after which she resolutely abandoned that duty. But there could be another explanation, which is that this supremely mated pair transcended physical love. Their true dwelling place was the mental plane of the spirit. They may have made the discovery that sex becomes transmuted at higher levels of conscious-ness, still holding all the excitement and lovingness of ordinary sexu-ality, but to a finer degree. Their deep satisfaction with each other over so many years is a clear indication of soul-satisfaction, which far supersedes the pleasures of the body.

We can be certain that their sexual energies were well and fully used, their masculine and feminine forces flowing into each other in the free exchange of the completed, androgenous being. Her intellect flowered, and his feeling self came into its own. Devoted to the service of humanity, rich in love for each other, they employed their matching talents in a single focus that had profound influence on society.

Upon her death, Mill claimed that the spring of his life was broken. She died in France, where she was buried, and he bought a house overlooking the cemetery. He spent more and more time there every year, and while in England he continued their work, knowing that she still guided his life.

His great consolation was Harriet's twenty-seven-year-old daughter, Helen Taylor, who was his companion for the rest of his life. He considered her the inheritor of much of Harriet's wisdom and all of her nobleness of character. "Surely," he wrote, "no one ever before was so fortunate as, after a loss such as mine, to draw another prize in the lottery of life—another companion, stimulator, advisor, and instructor of the rarest quality."

His love had a focus again and was able to express itself in a continued life of devotion. This was not a lottery prize he'd won, but a gift from the Divine Plan. We can be confident that Helen came to him from a near position in his and Harriet's group soul, just as Brahms was there to console Clara Schumann in her loss.

How significant it is that the man who led the thinkers of his generation possessed such a feminine love nature. He epitomizes the high level of the feminine in the evolved masculine soul. It is truly masculine to love greatly and have the courage to say so.

Elizabeth Barrett Browning's immortal sonnet to Robert might well have expressed Mill's feelings:

How do I love thee? Let me count the ways.
I love thee to the depth and breadth and height
My soul can reach, when feeling out of sight
For the ends of Being and ideal Grace.
I love thee to the level of every day's
Most quiet need, by sun and candle-light.
I love thee freely, as men strive for Right;
I love thee purely, as they turn from Praise.
I love thee with the passion put to use
In my old griefs, and with my childhood's faith.
I love thee with a love I seemed to lose
With my lost saints,—I love thee with the breadth,
Smiles, tears, of all my life!—and, if God choose,
I shall but love thee better after death.

Only a true poet is capable of expressing in words the high love of the soul. Early among these was Petrarch, the fourteenth-century poet laureate of Italy, whose sonnets to Laura are considered the greatest love poems ever written.

Petrarch first met the beautiful Laura on April 6, 1327. She died of the black plague twenty-one years later to the day. In his words: "Laura, illustrious by her own virtues and long celebrated in my poems, first appeared to my eyes in the earliest period of my manhood on the sixth day of April, anno Domini 1327, in the Church of St. Claire at Avignon, at the morning hour. And in the same city at the same hour of the same day in the same month of April, but in the year 1348, that light was withdrawn from our day."

From his first sight of her until his death she was the focusing passion of his life;

I have never been weary of this love,
My lady, nor shall I be while last my years.

In the final collection of Petrarch's verse were 366 poems, known in Italian by the generic name, *Rime.* The theme of the overwhelming majority of the *Rime* is his love for Laura, "in life and in death." The collection is divided into two parts, the first containing the poems written "In vita di Madonna Laura," the second, "In morte di Madonna Laura."

Historians believe that Laura was the daughter of a Provençal nobleman, Audibert de Noves, and married to Hugues de Sade. She mothered many children—some say eleven. That Petrarch's love for Laura was denied fulfillment in the common sense set the tone for his sonnets and songs. Above all, the *Rime* sings of the sad and woeful beauty of love, of the longing for the unattainable, of the rebellion against denial, of the inward laceration of the lover, and of his melancholic resignation. In the *Rime* all these moods of a lover have found their timeless representation. And the very fact that the figure of Laura is so idealized has made it possible for many readers of these sonnets to see in the image of Laura the picture of their own beloved, and to hear in the words of the poet the expression of their own thoughts and the echoes of their own love.

This may well have been the higher purpose in the arrangement that held these twin souls apart, if twins they were. If they were, we would expect to see a matching poetic gift in Laura; but the poetic talents of women were not publicly expressed in those times. Still, twins might incarnate expressly for one to inspire the other to great heights of artistry, for their own evolutionary benefit and that of the world—in this case to give utterance to the mute longings of so many through the centuries. Or again, Laura may not have been his twin but one a little more removed in the group soul, who struck a resonance within him that brought forth the passion for the absent twin, known to him in spiritual heights.

We do see repeated here the familiar twin pattern of attributing the best of oneself to one's counterpart. Petrarch wrote: "Whatever little I am, I have become through her. For if I possess any name and fame at all, I should never have obtained them unless she had cared with her most noble affection for the sparse seeds of virtues planted in my bosom by Nature."

"Laura's mind," he continues, "does not know earthly cares but burns with heavenly desires. Her appearance truly radiates beams of divine beauty. Her morals are an example of perfect uprightness. Neither her voice nor the force of her eyes nor her gait are those of an ordinary human being."

Petrarch asserted emphatically that he had "always loved her soul more than her body," though he admitted that, under the compulsion of love and youth, "occasionally I wished something dishonorable."

Eventually Petrarch succeeded in conquering himself, for he writes in the *Secretum*, composed in the form of a dialogue between himself and St. Augustine, his spiritual guide and conscience: "Now I know what I want and wish, and my unstable mind has become firm. She, on her part, has always been steadfast and has always stayed one and the same. The better I understand her womanly constancy, the more I admire it. If once I was grieved by her unyielding resolution, I am now full of joy over it and thankful."

In a later sonnet he expresses his profound gratitude:

I thank her soul and her holy device
That with her face and her sweet anger's bolts
Bid me in burning think of my salvation.

The climax of this love story is reached when Petrarch, inspired by the example of Laura's perfection, masters himself and his desires and begins to strive for the salvation of his soul. Eventually Laura assumes an ideal nature, as disclosed in one of the sonnets:

In what part of the sky, in what idea
Was the example from which Nature wrought
That charming lovely face wherein she sought
To show her power in the upper sphere?

This conception of Laura as the sublime ideal shows most clearly the transformation that Laura had undergone in the poet's mind: she has become the image of the concept of beauty, the embodiment of good and right. His perception of Laura's ultimate transfiguration is revealed in a later sonnet where his ...

... inner eye
Sees her soar up and with the angels fly
At the feet of our own eternal Lord.

His last, great unfinished work, the *Canzoniere,* is a symbolic vision of one man's story, raised from the autobiographical to the universal, the story of humanity in its progress from earthly passion to fulfillment in God. Love triumphs over the greatest men, but is captured by Chastity; which in its turn, in the person of Laura, is overcome by Death; which is conquered by glory, which is itself annihilated by Time: only in God does everything of beauty and everything of value, love for Laura and for glory, shine eternally beyond all space and time, and heaven and earth are reconciled according to Petrarch's noble and constant dream.

Not all twin souls rise to Petrarch's height of verbal grandeur. Modern language is simpler and more natural, easier for us to relate to. A twin-soul story within our own time has been beautifully rendered in the autobiography, *The Way Things Happen* by Ingaret Giffard, wife of the distinguished author, Laurens van der Post.

She writes of their first meeting, on a ship bound for South Africa, his homeland: "When we talked it was not as if we had only just met, but as though we had never been parted."

One afternoon they go down to his cabin and simply lie on his bunk with their arms around each other. Of this she writes:

It had not been an erotic indulgence; it had not been an expression of physical attraction. It was a human experience; but it was also something beyond human understanding. As I lay there in Laurens' arms I felt that somehow we had both put our personal signature at the bottom of one of the more closely-written pages of life itself. When at last we rose I knew that, although I was the same person, there was one profound difference. I was no longer alone: in fact I could never be alone again. Things would go wrong, of course, but when they did, and I could totally share the experience with another human being, that would change the texture of the calamity, because it could be contained in the rightness of our consummated communion. These were poor words, I knew, with which to express the feeling of life's inevitability, brought into being by our common self recognition.... It was a state of being and of belonging that was not in the world of ordinary affairs.

There is yet another level of twinship extending far beyond the world of ordinary affairs—yet with a surpassing world effect. That is the interaction between the Divine Father and the Divine Mother incarnated at the level of mastership. A towering example is Sri Aurobindo and his partner-guru, the Mother, who established their ashram at Pondicherry, India, in the 1920s. The work of these two rare beings, at their ashram and in their writings, conveys the sense of divinity that others perceived in them and that they worshipped in each other. Some Hindus believe that they were an incarnation of the Father and Mother aspects of God, Krishna, and Mahakali. In her childhood the Mother had visions of Aurobindo as Krishna. His teachings were centered upon her divinity as the Cosmic Mother, manifesting in different ways according to the plane upon which she is seen. At the same time, he wrote, "It is true of every soul on earth that it is a portion of the Divine Mother passing through the experiences of the Ignorance in order to arrive at the truth of its being and be the instrument of a Divine Manifestation and work here."

In truth, every pair of twin souls represents the Eternal Feminine and the Eternal Masculine, the Original Twins emergent from oneness. Through studying the lives of twin souls we arrive at a greater understanding of the God-force of love on which they are modeled. The identical pattern prevails in every pair, from the lowest status to the highest. We are given glimpses into the lives of Sri Aurobindo and the Mother in the book *Twelve Years with Sri Aurobindo,* by the Indian writer, Nirodbaran, "'The Two who are one,'" Nirodbaran quotes Aurobindo as saying, "'are the secret of all power. The Two who are one are the might and right in things.'" He continues:

> There used to be considerable speculation in the early days about their mutual relationship. Was it one of Master and disciple or Shiva and Shakti? I was therefore very curious from the start to observe and discern the relationship. I came to the conclusion that it was that of Shiva and Shakti. The Mother has said, "Without him, I exist not; without me he is unmanifest." And we were given the unique opportunity of witnessing the dual personality of the One enacting on our earth plane an immortal drama, rare in the spiritual history of man. I could perfectly realize that without the Mother, Sri Aurobindo's stupendous realisations could not have taken such a concrete shape on this terrestrial base. In fact, he was waiting for the Mother's coming. He said that with the Mother's help he covered ten years of sadhana in one year.

> They revered each other and deferred to each other in all things.

> If at any time we pressed our own opinion against the Mother's, Sri Aurobindo would pull us up saying, "You think Mother does not know?" Similarly, if Sri Aurobindo passed some remark, the Mother would accept it as the last word. We used to hear her remark, "Sri Aurobindo said so." And Sri Aurobindo would quote the Mother's authority. To both of them, the other's word was law. One of us observed that only two persons have realized and put into practice Sri Aurobindo's Yoga of surrender: the Mother surrendering to Sri Aurobindo and Sri Aurobindo to the Mother.

> They tended each other. The Mother was meticulous about every detail of his comfort, and he was equally solicitous about her well-being. He followed closely all her outer activities and enveloped her

with an aura of protection against the dark forces. He asserted very firmly that their life was a battleground in a very real sense, and that he and the Mother were actively waging a continuous war against the adverse forces. The Mother said once that illnesses in their case were more than usually difficult to cure because of the concentrated attack of the adverse forces. Yet they guarded each other against any harm that could be caused by those forces. Says Nirodbaran:

> Just as Sri Aurobindo used to protect the Mother, she protected him when needed: it was the role of the Lord and the Shakti. These are occult phenomena beyond our human intelligence.

They were the same, and yet complementary. The Mother's and Sri Aurobindo's talks were in vivid contrast.

> They sharply bring out the characteristics of two different personalities, though their consciousness is one.... Here the Mother's personality dominated the whole atmosphere; her tone, mood and manner were stamped with a seriousness, energy and force that demanded close attention.... The striking difference with Sri Aurobindo was his impersonality.... They were like a father and mother, both loving, but one indulgent, liberal, large, the other a firm though not inconsiderate disciplinarian. Both are aspects of the one Divine—Impersonal and Personal—and both have their ineffable charm.

The mutual surrender is characteristic of twin soulship, as is the protectiveness on both sides, the reverence for the being of the other, and the strong, unique, complementary characters founded on oneness. High aspiration and service, so perfectly illustrated in these twin masters, will always be found in the completed pair. Taken together, they form the picture of spiritual love.

Sri Aurobindo teaches that all manifestation has been brought into being and is sustained by the Feminine of God. To uplift the heart and soul to the Divine Mother, the Universal Goddess, is to touch the true source of female power. This is the message for our time.

Feminine power is the power of all-inclusive love. It is this and this alone which will heal the world, close the divisions between sexes and creeds, and end the separation of souls.

CHAPTER SIX

SEX AS TRANSCENDENCE

I T HAS BEEN SAID that the trouble with heaven is that there is no sex. How incompletely, then, is paradise conceived!

Sexual joy is not confined to earth; it ascends, as we ascend, into the higher worlds. The nearer heavens have been visited and reports brought back, as numerous near-death experiences attest. It is known that there is, in fact, a higher sexuality. The difference between it and the lower, or purely physical, is this: ecstatic feelings can be induced in the body through sexual excitation even when love is absent; sometimes, even when loathing is present. Higher sexuality, in contrast, is entirely dependent upon love. It occurs only when accompanied by genuine, kindred love between the two participants.

Higher sexual joys are by no means restricted to the upper regions of the spirit world. With the increasing enlightenment that marks our time in human evolution, sexuality is undergoing a change. There is a trend away from genitally-focused sex toward a sacred sexuality, which admits the spirit to the temple of the body in its rituals of love. This is a total cellular involvement manifesting in a thrillingness and out-bursting love through the entire body. It contrasts with the loneliness and alienation that so often follow orgasmic-driven sex, which itself is a contributing factor to a great many of the problems between men and women.

It seems that the forces of Light are at last claiming this energy as their own; for sex energy is the love energy of the Divine in manifestation. Flowing forth in the beginning, the love-force created and infilled the cosmos. It remained obedient to the will of its Creator through the evolving phases of material life, until reaching the human level. There the love energy met two major obstructions: human free will, and the efforts of the dark forces to sabotage the Plan of return.

The two combined to contaminate the pure sex energy, the love energy, with selfishness, cruelty, and the drive for power. Sex and love broke apart. The split was always intended, as part of the duality by which the human soul learns and grows. Also intended was that love and sex will reunite to become pure love energy again, through the alchemy of spiritually aware human beings. In the reuniting, something will have been added. Just as the division of the twin souls and their return to wholeness brings added dimension to God, so will the light and dark sexual powers combine in a new and great light of love. Indeed the surpassing joys of sexuality in the higher worlds may be a direct outgrowth of this earthly struggle.

The shift of sexuality from the shadow realm toward its rightful place in the sun will not be accomplished overnight. The wedge between sex and love has been driven deep by the dark powers, which, from the beginning of time, have seized upon sex as a source of misery exactly proportionate to its power for bliss. Misery and bliss have always been bed companions. Our history of wars and humanitarian invention reflect these dueling forces of the cosmos. Sex expressed through the emotions and the body is given impetus by superordinate spiritual and psychic forces, benign or malignant. Always they are under the control of a directing intelligence, whose motive is to further evolution or retard it.

The higher intelligences align themselves with love, while those below align with the opposite, darker emotions, which they deliberately generate for their own perverted self-satisfaction. For the most part these are spirits of the lower astral, who have misused their free will in life and have passed over with darkened minds and twisted emotions. Death has thwarted them in their physical hungers. They continue to crave the satisfaction of their individual lusts, and to seek gratification by invading the bodies and minds of living men. They select persons with like appetites, whom they pull down into further defilement of this sacred energy. The entities themselves, lacking will and individuation, have become the minions of the directing authorities of evil.

The minions are of low intelligence, but the higher-ups, the highest of the low, are cunning, ever planning the strategies in the eternal contest for the human will. For it is the will that chooses between good and evil. We see in this the nature of possession as opposed to inspiration. The aim of the dark forces is to invade and possess, to sap entirely the will of the one who has submitted. Advanced spiritual beings do not possess; they guide, they stand back, transmitting light from their high sources, encouraging the exercise of free will in those they would inspire.

They inspire us most particularly in our acts of love. The sexual act is known to be a holy union, that which George Eliot (Marian Evans) has termed "the deepest and gravest joy in human experience." Yet this joy is not the ultimate. It is a step toward higher sexual joys, in earthly life but especially in the worlds beyond. The following twin-soul history illustrates the next stage of sexuality: sex as transcendence.

Alexandra and Leroy were both musicians. Leroy was a virtuoso violinist, constantly on tour. Alexandra was married, with three children. A pianist by training, she taught the instrument to her three children and other students. The meeting occurred after she attended one of Leroy's concerts. At the end of the performance Alexandra was seized with an overwhelming urge to go backstage and speak to him.

She did so, and as they shook hands, she felt as if she had known him all her life. His eyes carried the same message. It was evidence of the ancient link, the deep connection of individual souls recalling a once-undivided Self. Twin love grew rapidly, but the circumstances were not conducive to its full consummation. Alexandra, though not completely fulfilled in her marriage, had loyalties to her family which she could not in conscience abandon. Leroy was unattached but wedded to his work, locked into an extended concert schedule.

In spite of his busy schedule, Leroy began to phone Alexandra from all his concert stops. After their initial meeting they met again briefly and infrequently, yet grew in closeness as they talked long-distance and expressed themselves in letters. Their bond strengthened through the compatibilities of mind, emotions, and spirit as they were uncovered and revealed. While accepting the limitations of their outer circumstances, they reached toward each other with growing fervor.

Nothing stands still, certainly not love that is released from long confinement. There is an expansion of being that accompanies soul love, and no force on earth can confine it. Both Alexandra and Leroy are mystical and spiritually aware people, yet well grounded in the practical conduct of their lives. But things were happening beyond the periphery of earthly life. Spiritual forces were at work both within and without. The meeting of souls is serious business to Those who oversee the intertwining fates in the great patterns of Return. A soul union, which is destined, will fulfill itself in the best possible way for all whose lives are touched by it, as long as those involved remain open to their center of truth, their intuition, the channel to the highest good.

By whatever means deemed necessary, the soul *will* have its way. If intolerable restrictions are present, it will break through with supersensory powers for those in whom it dwells, always provided that they are ready for such powers. The force of the soul is the same that drives the great cataracts of Nature. It cannot be stopped by any law but its own. The only human force that can stand up to it is genuine morality.

The first intimations of powers beyond the ordinary that Alexandra experienced was her response to Leroy's voice. After speaking with him on the phone, she would find herself suffused with radiant energy, an energy previously felt only in the exaltation of great music or rare heights of meditation. The energy built as the bond between them grew. After they had talked, Alexandra found that she lay awake the entire night in a mysterious joy and elevation of mind, passing into timelessness so that the night seemed all too short. She compared it with past insomnia, when every minute seemed an hour and every hour a night. Now she watched the light rise over the sill all too soon, just as it had at Juliet's window. Though her lover was not with her, the power of his love was communicating itself to her as if he were.

The infusion of energy was so great that it remained throughout the following day. She had discovered something more restorative than sleep. It was love energy, the energy of the cosmos. It was sex energy, reunited with its birth stream, love: love and sex transcendent.

Each telephone conversation produced one of these peak experiences. For two or three nights in a row Alexandra could forego sleep. She described the sensation as "an expansion of myself into a huge force field composed of light and swirling color. The feeling was of vibrant activity, like a dance of atoms that I could plainly see, for I felt as though I had become transparent. It was bliss, I was made of bliss, and I understood that every atom of everything is made of bliss. At times I was transported into a great stillness, when all the atoms came to a perfect stand still. The bliss was even greater in the stillness. I stopped breathing so as not to shatter it, and remembered, *Be still and know that I am God.* I could have stayed in it forever. Even as I say it, I know I will be in it forever, and Leroy with me, and everyone else that we have ever loved, for it seemed to spread to the farthest reaches of the Universe. I describe it so poorly for what it really was!"

And what was it really? There is little doubt that Alexandra was experiencing a spontaneous opening of the chakra centers and a flow of kundalini. Chakras are energy centers that exist within the human energy field for the purpose of absorbing, transforming, and distributing the universal energy, called prana or chi. There are seven main chakras: the root center, located at the base of the spine; the sacral center, in the sexual-genital region; the navel center, or solar plexus; the heart chakra; the throat chakra; the frontal chakra, located between the eyebrows; and the crown chakra, at the top of the head. Kundalini, the universal power transmitted to and through the human being, is thought of as the serpent power coiled at the base of the spine. On being aroused, it flows through the chakras to the brain, bringing with it a tremendous energy, which can result in enlightenment or, if improperly handled, madness. Kundalini is thus the basic spiritual energy of the earth, the power that drives Creation.

Normally the kundalini and chakra energies are stimulated into activity through specific yoga disciplines. Alexandra had practiced none of these, except meditation. Her experience revealed that the energy system can spring open under the stimulus of love. Her spiritual opening closely resembled the sudden, overwhelming advent of cosmic consciousness into the mind and soul.

The consciousness that we call cosmic consciousness arrives at the instant of readiness. It is the God-consciousness that dwells in all things. This awareness is accompanied by a bliss uncontainable by the human mind, and thus the mind is forced to expand in a single instant to what seems like broad reaches of the cosmos. It should be stated that not all cases of cosmic consciousness are by way of this grand seizure; some arrive in a relatively minor fashion, yet leave the subject changed for life. The recorded cases of such illumination have been thoroughly researched by Dr. William Bucke, and are well described in his book, *Cosmic Consciousness.*

Then Alexandra found that clairvoyant faculties, never experienced before, were unfolding swiftly. Awakening suddenly one night, she had a startling vision. She described it to Leroy in a letter:

It was a vision, but it was a happening, too. I was in it and observing it all at once. I saw you in a spiritual realm. I was there, standing near you, watching as a river of golden light poured into you through the top of your head. It poured and poured. I was astonished at your capacity for this light. It seemed it would never stop. But then it did. You looked at me and took a step toward me. I stepped toward you. Then we simply flowed into each other. You entered me; I entered you, wholly and in every part. We became one body, and with this came a rapture that doubled me over in my bed, for I felt it physically, in every fragment of my being. It was so real that when daylight arose a few hours later it seemed that it rose upon an artificial world.

This visionary experience proved to be an initiation into astral travel. Not long afterward, as Alexandra was getting into bed—she and her husband slept in separate rooms—she suddenly saw Leroy standing there at the foot. The sight scarcely surprised her; it seemed completely natural. She said inwardly and calmly, "Oh, there's Leroy," as though he had just entered her room in person. She attributed the naturalness to the knowledge that they were one in spirit. In our spiritual dimension there is no space, and so he was easily present in astral form.

In her experience they made love. Alexandra described the lovemaking as close to physical, their astral bodies duplicating the physical movements with great passion and exchange of love, verbal and telepathic. Penetration was not localized, but a complete fusion of their spirit bodies took place. The effect for Alexandra was an exquisite thrillingness throughout her whole body, including the sexual zones, coupled with high spiritual joy and pleasure.

The event moved into timelessness—which later proved to be two hours by the clock—and continued with intensity and exaltation, yet mixed with a spreading peacefulness and calm. The great discovery was that peace, rather than excitement, brought forth the purest bliss.

In place of physical orgasm, the bliss took wing; Alexandra experienced a tremendous lifting effect, a soaring, as though, she said, together she and Leroy were jetting into the cosmos "like a shooting star silently exploding, sending down a shower of sparks which washed around us in spirals of indescribable, soft sensation, swelling the heart and illumining the mind." This was followed by the pure stillness of contemplation, as described by the high mystics.

Here is the sacred sexuality, the transcendent spiritual sex, which does not deny the body but more fully engages it, opening from it greater founts of ecstasy. This is the sex of the future; already there in the spiritual realms, it is being initiated now, from our base on earth. It is not reserved for twin souls, but does wear a Reserved sign for those who are open to their souls and to the power of love.

All of it was happening within Alexandra's consciousness and no doubt in Leroy's higher consciousness. It entered his brain-memory only at one point: Alexandra had felt her attention drawn to the clock and had noted the hour, eleven, just before seeing Leroy in her room. The next evening, talking with him on the telephone, separated again by earthly miles, she told him what had happened and wondered if he remembered. He did not, but asked, "What time was that?" Then he added quickly, "Don't tell me ! Wait a minute ... eleven o'clock! At eleven o'clock I thought about visiting you."

"That's exactly when you appeared," said Alexandra with a sense of wonder.

Their enforced separation had forced their souls to break through the boundaries of time and space. Once broken, the boundaries could not contain them again. Nor would their love ever become routine. Where love and sex becomes monotonous and finally boring, it is because a partnership is grounded; it is moving horizontally instead of vertically. The love of twin souls has a cosmic purpose. The purpose is advancement, ascendence, the transmutation of the lower to the higher.

As Alexandra and Leroy's bond continued strengthening and seeking expression, it moved upward from one stage to the next. Leroy, the initiator, came to her in his bodies of finer substance, elevating her to the awakening of her own. At first Alexandra was able to actually see his astral form. There were a few such astral visits, and each time she saw him clearly placed in the room, moving to her across physical space. But that soon changed, and she saw him only in her mind; she knew his presence intuitively, and from the sensations of their union. These sensations became more and more refined, delicate and subtle, though as powerful, even more so, in their effect.

An ascension was taking place within them both. It was detectable not by the yardsticks of science but by the continually elevating consciousness that finally will be the measure of all things. They were learning to employ their bodies of finer substance, to acquaint themselves with the temples of the spiritual life, wherein ecstasy is the rule, not the exception.

The first of the finer vehicles is the etheric body, which duplicates and interpenetrates the physical, and does not leave it until the moment of death. Next is the astral body, which is free to travel and, in fact, departs during sleep. Highly evolved people, such as the spiritual masters, can send their astral forms abroad on specific missions, while in waking consciousness they remain occupied with physical activities. A finer body is the mental body. Although our soul in its full dimension dwells simultaneously on every plane, the three lower worlds of the physical, astral, and mental are all we can grasp at the human stage. Beyond the mental we will graduate to awareness of higher and more subtle bodies still, which we name the intuitive, the atmic, and the monadic, but cannot yet comprehend.

It seems evident from Alexandra and Leroy's experience that one or more of the bodies beyond the astral come into play in spiritual lovemaking. Physical indications may be present, as well. Alexandra received two unmistakable physical, sensory signals of Leroy's presence. One was a gentle activation and closing over of the throat. This points to an evolutionary move. Eventually the energies of the lower chakras in the body must be transmuted and lifted up to the higher. A vital step is the raising of the sacral (reproductive) energy to the throat chakra, signifying the transmutation of the process of physical procreation to that of creative expression. In Alexandra the activating of the throat chakra was a spiritual-sexual response to the presence of the twin soul.

Her second sensory sign was the "breeze." In *The Secret Doctrine*, H.P. Blavatsky informs us that a spirit visiting a sensitive person will be felt as a passing breeze. It was this breeze playing over Alexandra's lips, eyes, and hands that let her know, even before the mental communion began, that he was there.

No words, she says, can express the beauty and the bliss of these encounters. Nevertheless, she continually attempted to describe them in her letters to Leroy, as the visits occurred for the most part when he was asleep and vacating his physical body. He had no clear recollection of them, as we have little or no recollection of our visits to the spirit plane in sleep. Yet we are given flashes of memory, and Leroy, too, had intimations and reverberations that reached his consciousness.

On one occasion he awoke suddenly in the night to sense himself soaring through cosmic spaces, joined with Alexandra. When he spoke to her the following evening he found that she had been experiencing a "visitation" at the exact same hour. On other occasions he saw her floating above his bed as a Chagall angel and felt a slight breeze on his lips. One afternoon as she lay down to rest, Alexandra was surprised to feel the breeze on her face, along with other signs of his presence.

She took note of the time and asked Leroy about it that evening. They discovered that during the precise time of her nap he had been half dozing on a train, having just read a letter from her that he was carrying in his breast pocket.

The couple had a number of such synchronicities, enough to convince them that they were living a twin-soul reality and building a bridge between this and the higher worlds. It is a bridge that many others will construct. As time goes on, there will be a flowing traffic between the worlds, or through the spaces of this one, empowering lovers in all circumstances, those held apart by distance, by physical infirmity, or by the illusory separation we call death.

There is much to be discovered about the sexuality that spans the known and nebulous realms. With Alexandra and Leroy we cannot be sure why it was he who took the initiative of astral travel, unless it is simply because the yang initiating impulse is stronger in the masculine soul. Alexandra's receptivity depicts the feminine principle. It is possible that she traveled to him also in her sleep, as implied by his angel visions, and he was not as open as she to receive the experience.

Night visits between souls occur the world over, and almost always the memory is excluded from the waking mind. After the passing over of Sri Aurobindo, while the Mother was still in her earthly body, the following was reported by a disciple in the ashram: "We have now learned from the Mother that Sri Aurobindo has built a home in the subtle-physical plane and many of us visit him at night in our subtle bodies. She has often told us that we visit her or she visits us, during our sleep. In the morning she has often asked, 'Do you know anything about it?' "

Fortunately we have the record of a few like Alexandra, who have received the visits while awake. The purpose that lies behind events reveals itself here: these two people pioneered the lovemaking of the future. There is no doubt in Alexandra's mind that spiritual love-making is sacred sexuality and superior to physical sex by far. The complete union that is possible to spirit bodies is that for which everyone yearns, and seeks in the joinings of the flesh. This explains the disappointment and letdown that so often follow the physical act of sex. The soul carries the vision but the body does not fulfill it, despite its moment or two of glory.

In contrast, let us listen to Alexandra as she described for Leroy one of their spiritual love meetings, encounters that occurred weekly, or several times a week, over many years:

> It is always different, new, original, creative, like each new day. I have learned to be completely open and receptive and allow you to set the tone. At the beginning there is the breeze on my face, intensifying around the mouth, often felt inside it, or around my feet underneath the covers—sometimes in the bath! Yes, the breeze under the water! How thrilling it is to see natural laws broken by themselves. But even before the breeze there is a knowing, a certainty of your presence, slow-gathering in my mind. It expands my heart and sends warmth flowing through my veins. It is high, high excitement, yet a peaceful excitement with no tension in it. Always there comes the quiet seizure in the throat. It is your speech to mine, your creative soul speaking a thousand words a second, all of them beautiful with love.
>
> Then your spirit body acts on me in ways so thrilling, so

varied and creative, that I hold my breath! Breath stops, the way it does in meditation, or so it seems. I sink into the feelings and observe them all at once. It rouses in me an *attentiveness* so acute that I think Nature must feel like this in bringing round the sun!

Sometimes you lift my spirit right out of me; I feel you lifting it, so tenderly, like a mother gently raising a child up from its cradle. As this happens I become keenly aware of your spirit body, its racing vibrations, its brilliant colors. Then all of these stream into me, passing through and through me in waves of rapture. And I respond with the passion of my liberated spirit. We engage each other, ah, how we engage! … like foamings of the sea or the sparkling, tumbling waters of a fountain. I will never get used to the passage of time as this happens, two hours or more as a rule, never less than two. When I finally glance at the clock I can't believe what it is telling me, for I have been in timelessness, in eternity. The hours have passed like minutes. And I am hungry! I get up and make some tea and sit a long time sipping it, watching the snow or the rain or the moon through the french windows, remembering … unable to sleep and not wanting to.

As we go on, you refine the methods. Last night you introduced a variation on one which you have used before and which I love … but this time with a stroke of genius. Immediately on coming to me, gradually but swiftly you moved into me, filling me up completely with your being. I felt your life within me, very still, as though waiting. Then came the faintest stirring in the solar plexus, and after that a touch, a whispering touch, traveling slowly, infinitely slowly down the center of my legs, lightly, like the delicate etchings of frost on windowpanes. These fragile sensations entered each of my toes in turn, going to the very tip of each, then appeared in my arms, down through hands and fingers, the thrillingness gathering through the very delicacy of it. This went on all through my body, and when it reached my head I even had the feeling it was being drawn along each separate hair! And when every inch had been covered with this infinitely gentle, loving touch, then ... *then* your power surged! You became a flowing, pulsing radiance within me, all of your magnetism compressed into my exact shape and size. You became my very life; I was like someone who had been only a shell, an empty skin, and had now leapt to livingness.

That livingness we shared was pure ecstasy, an almost unbearable ecstasy. I spoke your name and cried out my love, my body twisting and moving. I felt it graceful like a joyous creature of the wild. I was part of the cosmic movement, all the actions of love concentrated in me. I became truly aware, for the first time, of the absolute oneness of our souls. No longer were we two lovers acting upon one another, two beings consorting together, but one bliss weaving back and forth within itself.

This is the true experience of heaven. You have brought me to it. How can I speak my adoration? It's the adoration of God, God in thee, and of the sure promise that it will be like this for everyone. In my joy I feel some of the joy of everyone, the joy locked up within them as it used to be in me, but present, even now all present!—simply waiting, as I waited for you and you for me.

Let me describe it more from this earthly perspective. It is impossible to convey, and yet it must be attempted, I feel. This is not just an ecstasy of mind! This is thoroughly physical, a sensation as of pure golden sunlight spreading open all the fibers of the body and filling them up with pleasure—something beyond pleasure, the very source of pleasure. It emits rays of itself into the cosmos and receives them back in a swoon of gratitude. It is subtly, excruciatingly orgiastic, as if the entire physical structure trembles on the very edge of that precipice. This is because it is being experienced in the body as well as engaging all the other finer vehicles. It is total. It wants nothing but to remain, to be, to continue; it is sufficient to itself. It is perfect peace and being-ness.

In trying to communicate to him the peace that always followed their communions, Alexandra called on the words of William E. Channing who wrote, early in the nineteenth century:

Peace is the highest and most strenuous action of the soul, but an entirely harmonious action, in which all our powers and affections are blended in a beautiful proportion, and sustain and perfect one another. It is more than silence after storms. It is as the concord of all melodious sounds.... It is a conscious harmony with God and the creation ... an alliance of love with all beings, a sympathy with all that is pure and happy, a surrender of every separate will and interest, a participation of the spirit and life of the universe, an entire concord of purpose with its Infinite Original. This is peace and the true happiness of man and woman.

Alexandra continued:

And that isn't all. After our lovemaking last night—a true "making of cosmic love"—I slept awhile and dreamed, feeling myself floating in a sea of peace. Then I awoke with a remembered vision of a place I had just left. There I had been watching tall, thin El Greco-like figures composed of light moving softly and purposefully about, with infinite grace and beauty. They must have been made of very very fine substance, for they were bathed in an ineffable softness that made them barely distinguishable from the light all around them. But I will never forget them, and I knew they were real, as real as yourself in your radiant spiritual being. And it was you, your presence and your creatively expressing love, which led me to the place where they live and move, and where they showed themselves to my inspired sight.

Here we witness the transmutation of sexual energy to higher and higher peaks of consciousness and joy. Who could deny that sexuality fills the heavens? It also remains our greatest gift on earth, as we learn its holy uses and sort out and discard its darker ones. Spiritual lovemaking is a union of earth and heaven. This is part of the New Age of synthesis. With the deepening dimensions in our outlook, we can appreciate the broad applications of sex transcendent. It is expressed in Leroy's spirit visiting Alexandra in her body; or in loving sexual intercourse, which allows the spirit full involvement; or between two spirits, one incarnate and the other in spirit life.

There have been reports of spirit-sexual encounters in some books on astral travel, but its dangers are seldom mentioned. To project oneself out into the astral world looking for love is rather like walking naked down a dark alley late at night. The astral air is crowded with spirits untrustworthy and even dangerous. For one's protection there must be a focus: a person known in this life, or a beloved partner who has passed over to the other side. Two people with established bonds of love and harmony, if spiritually developed, may well be able to span the worlds and unite their spirits in acts of love. No doubt it has been happening through the ages, in dreams or the unconsciousness of sleep, and goes largely unrecognized. These ideas are not new. They are at least as old as Greek mythology, fore-shadowed in the love between gods and humans.

We are now in a time of recognition, when the archetypes are rising into consciousness and finding application in our lives. The spiritual partnership has become a reality, not only between twin souls, but others as well. Gary Zukav writes of this in his best-selling book, *The Seat of the Soul:*

> An archetype is a collective human idea. The archetype of marriage was designed to assist physical survival. When two people marry, they participate in an energy dynamic in which they merge their lives in order to help each other survive physically. The archetype of marriage is no longer functional. It is being replaced with a new archetype that is designed to assist spiritual growth. This is the archetype of spiritual, or sacred, partnership.
>
> The underlying premise of a spiritual partnership is a sacred commitment between the partners to assist each other's spiritual growth. Spiritual partners recognize their equality. Spiritual partners are able to distinguish personality from soul, and, therefore,

they are able to discuss the dynamics between them, their inter-actions, on a less emotionally-bound ground than husbands and wives. That ground does not exist within the consciousness of marriage. It exists only within the consciousness of spiritual part-nership because spiritual partners are able to see clearly that there is indeed a deeper reason why they are together, and that reason has a great deal to do with the evolution of their souls.

Because spiritual, or sacred, partners can see from this perspective, they engage in a very different dynamic than do husbands and wives. The conscious evolution of the soul is not part of the structural dynamic of marriage. It does not exist within that evolution, because when the evolutionary archetype of marriage was created for our species, the dynamic of conscious spiritual growth was far too mature a concept to be included.

What makes a spiritual, or sacred, partnership is that the souls within the partnership understand that they are together in a committed relationship, but the commitment is not to physical security. It is rather to be with each other's physical lives as they reflect spiritual consciousness.

The bond between spiritual partners exists as real as it does in marriage, but for significantly different reasons. Spiritual part-ners are not together in order to quell each other's financial fears or because they can produce a house in the suburbs and that entire conceptual framework.... The commitment of spiritual partners is to each other's spiritual growth, recognizing that that is what each of them is doing on Earth, and that everything serves that.

Spiritual partners bond with an understanding that they are together because it is appropriate for their souls to grow together. They recognize that their growth may take them to the end of their days in this incarnation and beyond, or it may take them six months. They cannot say that they will be together forever. The duration of their partnership is determined by how long it is appropriate for their evolution to be together. All the vows that a human being can take cannot prevent the spiritual path from exploding through and breaking those vows if the spirit must move on. It is appropriate for spiritual partners to remain together only as long as they grow together…. Just as external power is no longer appropriate to our evolution, the archetype of marriage is no longer appropriate. This does not mean that the institution of marriage will disappear overnight.

Marriages will continue to exist, but marriages that succeed will only succeed with the consciousness of spiritual partnership.

Now comes the question: What is to be done when a true soul partner, twin or otherwise, comes into the life of a person already established in a conventional marriage? People must consult their souls, knowing that each situation is unique to their life-path and that each is for the purpose of ascension.

One man, caught in just such a triangle, sought the advice of his spiritual master, saying, "It's all such a puzzle. I can't see the solution." The master replied, "Don't look for the solution. Look at the puzzle. When you have found what the puzzle has to teach you, the solution will have presented itself."

The patterns are as varied as the people themselves. Some marriages survive, some break up, and some are shaken and reassembled along new lines. Whichever it is, we can know that the crisis serves the growth of every person in it and is designed according to what each has yet to learn. No one can break up a marriage that ought to continue, for marriages are maintained or dissolved according to soul needs and the karmic plan. If a marriage dissolves there is pain, and the pain is part of the purpose. The Plan always contains the challenges that each individual path requires in its progress through life. Because the Plan is sculpted around the greatest eventual good for all persons involved, they are guided every step of the way. The best and only true guidance comes from within each individual as admitted from the high Self by way of intuition. Those partners in life who are also soul partners are practiced at opening their intuition, for they have had to raise their spiritual energies in order to come together. As they are committed to each other's spiritual growth, they are committed also to the growth of those around them. And so they create a network of aid to include the family members who may have to find a new balance in the light of their partnership. The coming together of Alexandra and Leroy naturally had an effect on her family. Her children benefitted from her new found joy, but between her husband and herself there was tension. She recognized the need for them to find a new balance, and it was a matter that only time could resolve.

Who is the soul partner likely to be if not the twin? Most certainly soul partners are close kin of a group soul. They are brought together to inspire their further evolution toward their twins and to serve the purpose of Planetary Life. The planet itself is a great body of manifestation, an evolving Being: the planetary Logos. The chakra centers of the human being mirror the planetary centers. The entire sex aspect of manifestation in the different kingdoms of Nature expresses the energy of the Logos flowing through that center in Its body which corresponds to the generative organs. We aid planetary evolution as we raise our energies through our chakra centers and body sheaths. In a reciprocal flow the Logos sustains and uplifts us in the transmutation of our desire for union to more expanded and blissful ways.

The raising of the sexual energy is paralleled by an ascendence of the planetary inhabitants, the great cycling races of evolving humans. The Age of Lemur is the earliest human race of which we have any knowledge, and we know that the Lemurians were very much occupied with the lowest chakra, the sacral center. People of that time were close to the animal stage of evolution and were learning to inhabit their bodies and develop their sexual apparatus. They became overindulgent in the pleasures of the body and were in fact destroyed by the excesses that they visited upon themselves. Such diseases of excess as syphilis finally caused their race to die out.

The Lemurians, with their emphasis on the physical, were followed by the inhabitants of the lost continent of Atlantis. It was the task of the Atlanteans to evolve the astral body, that vehicle of feeling and emotion. The Atlanteans also went too far; in their pursuit of emotional pleasure they gave way to avarice and greed, and were brought down by their own selfishness.

Present humanity is occupied with evolving its mental powers. The mental body is far more than a vehicle of thought and intellectualization. It is a more precious carrier of the soul than any that have gone before. Love and intelligence are embodied here in one. The mind, with all its powers, moves into increasingly higher realization and expression. The lower emotions are outgrown. The higher feelings, with their essence of love-wisdom, are released. As pure mind contacts pure mind, the union is nothing less than soul to soul. That union can be experienced here and now. Soul-to-soul connection is finding its place in our daily lives and will become the norm as we advance.

Deep friendships are a melding of souls. So can be the connection between therapist and patient. One psychiatrist tells us that as he moves into deeper and deeper empathy with his patients, they both settle into a kind of altered state. Such a state induces a near telepathic transmission, a sensing within the therapist of what is happening within the patient. At the same time the patient becomes sensitive to the postures, gestures, and voice inflections of the therapist. This kind of sensitivity goes well beyond the level of physical perception and into the realm of the intuitive.

The breakthrough of Alexandra and Leroy, in their reach to one another, is an illustration of human capacity extended beyond itself. Yet every human being has this capacity. Coiled within each of us is the kundalini power, which, when released, will gather all the body/spirit forces into one fused and blended stream of energy. This was the energy directed toward Alexandra by her twin, and actively received by her. The infusion of power, transmitted to her repeatedly across vast geographical distances, caused her etheric body to intensify its vitality, and the physical body to be galvanized and energized. Her entire aura was co-ordinated and illumined, allowing her spirit form to withdraw in full waking consciousness and unite with Leroy's in the pure and sacred lovemaking of the higher planes.

This is sexual energy in its transcendent expression, the one force manifesting in all forms, empowered by love: love between twin souls, between doctor and patient, parent and child, teacher and pupil, friend and friend. It is the energy that keeps the wheeling systems in their places while continually expanding their reach toward the limitless, the high mirroring of our own expanding love.

CHAPTER SEVEN

RECOGNIZING THE TWIN

There is an old song that goes:

> They asked me how I knew
> my true love was true.
> I of course replied,
> 'Something here inside
> cannot be denied.'

Is this how it will be when our twin soul comes along? Will it be a sudden, illuminating flash, a feeling that truly cannot be denied? For some it will be. As one woman said about the introduction to her twin soul, "The minute I saw him I knew he was the other side of myself." And for her, this proved to be so.

We hear many such romantic versions of the meeting between two people, and often the pair are loosely called "soulmates." "Soulmates" is not a precise term, however; it can as easily mean a group soulmate as a twin soulmate. A person can have many soulmates but only one twin soul.

The notion of love at first sight is a popular one; your eyes meet across a crowded room and you just *know*. It *can* happen that way on first seeing the twin. But just as often, such a meeting of the eyes signals only sexual desire, a prelude to fleeting infatuation.

When the true twin is encountered, we don't necessarily know this at a first glance, yet we know ... something. The meeting has a certain intensity. The soul recognizes its own, even though it may take time for the recognition to reach the surface.

There was the instance of a man sitting casually in a lecture audience, when another rose to his feet and aggressively challenged the woman at the podium. The first man, a scientist, not given to emotional outbursts, whirled in his seat and countered the attack. A heated debate ensued. The scientist gave no ground. When he had subdued his opponent, he turned his eyes again to the speaker, who in the course of time he was to perceive as his twin soul. She named him her knight. They never forgot the drama of their meeting.

Drama may well attend the twin-soul encounter, for the story itself is the essence of drama. God is the supreme dramatist, after all. Another such meeting is described by a woman who was a nurse in the agricultural department of a university. One afternoon at five, as she prepared to lock the drug cupboard, "in came this scruffy-looking guy in filthy jeans, saying to me, 'Just leave it unlocked.' I got fire in my eye and snapped at him, 'My job is to lock the cupboard *and I'm locking it!*'" She locked it forcibly and walked out with her head in the air. Says he, "All the time I was trying to figure how to ask her out, but I didn't know how to pronounce her name—Moira." Later she discovered that he was one of the doctors in the department, a veterinary surgeon. Their subsequent marriage was extraordinarily happy, their children most beautiful and unique. Of him, she says, "He has wonderful feminine qualities and he always encourages me in using my masculine ones." There is the sign!

Twin souls can know each other by their basic samenesses and their balanced complementary differences. These do not show all at once. Realization of twinship is a process, an adventure in discovery, opening into a steadily widening angle of recognition. Acquaintanceship ripens quickly into friendship as the twins follow their star, which has guided them from the beginning. They have followed it by separate and diverse paths. Now its twin beams, illumining their paths, have become a single light. Their growing bond is a continuation, replication, and recovery of the ancient bond.

Recognition grows as their mutuality is revealed. The ground of their being is a shared one; they are two sides of the same soul, though with separate identities within it. Their sameness is most clearly revealed in the level of their spiritual vision. Thomas Carlyle wrote: "The chief thing about a man is what he thinks about this Universe of ours." Now, of course, we know that this applies to women, too; therefore this "chief thing" is matched in twin souls. They are like two people standing at the same place on the mountain, surveying the same panorama, which varies only in detail. The differing details are complementary. For instance, one twin may have a strictly focused vision, while the other ranges widely. This adds to each other's vision. The twin souls continually complete and complement, bringing new insights and inspirations to one another.

Sameness is revealed in compatibility of cultural taste, especially in music, the most highly spiritual of the arts. When divergence in taste exists it serves to broaden the other's path of learning and is accepted as such. Twin-soul partners share the same brand of humor, the same tastes in food, and similar social skills. Both may like cold weather or hot; both may love the sea or the mountains. For some, these combine in a general love of nature. Other twins both prefer city life, the proximity to the arts and the pulse of the nation.

Their handwriting shows unmistakable similarities, for graphology is a great revealer of character. The life-map of the palm is similarly etched in each, possibly with a matching line of Mars, of intuition, of mental power. If one twin is an early riser, the other will not be a lie-abed. Such habits speak deeply of character. The two likely have a similar physiognomy and certainly the same disposition. If one is sweet-natured, so is the other. It is, in fact, axiomatic that twin souls are good-natured, for the higher the spiritual evolution, the more joyful the spirit.

Temperaments are aligned in accordance with the four tempers: choleric, sanguine, melancholic, and phlegmatic. One twin pair, for example, showed a typical blend of sameness and balancing oppositeness: both were strongly choleric, with none of the phlegmatic; as for the remaining two tempers, one twin tended toward the sanguine

and the counterpart to the melancholic, the complementary opposite nature. There are countless small matchings. Punctuality is one
example. Both may be left-handed, or have similar physical disabili-
ties, stomach disorders or perhaps esophageal weakness. They are
twins, and the twinning runs throughout their life, in thoughts and
physical makeup. While we know of no relation between identical
twins and twin souls, the latter's underlying similarities find a
parallel in the case of identical twins who are separated in infancy
and adopted by different parents. If they meet as adults, they often
find that they dress the same, cut their hair the same way, are
engaged in the same kind of work, and show other similar inclina-
tions, even to the extent of having married the same kind of person.

We all know the surge of pleasure that comes with discovering
compatibilities with another. Thus is sounded the echoes of the
spirit, which constantly seeks its own reflection and quickly detects
the vision of union. The compatibilities sing the promise of return.
The flush of joy at their uncovering springs from the same source in
friend, group soul, or twin soul. The joy is most acute in the twin
souls because the corresponding characteristics cover the entire
canvas of their lives.

A large section of the canvas is taken up with their lifework. Probably the main signifying feature of twin-soulship, aside from gender
balance, is the occupation in which they are found. Each has chosen,
or been chosen by, some branch of the same work. The picture may
not be as clear-cut as with the Curies, the Brownings, and the Schumanns; there is always room for variation. It may be that both deal in
language, one in spoken language, the other in written. In such a
case the speaker would have a gift for writing, and the writer, for
speaking. Beneath the words, both would be driven by the same
compelling interest, a fascination, perhaps, with all that makes the
human mechanism work. As their lives interconnect, their experience converges, leading into combined work of higher fulfillment.

Both may be healers, in different areas of the healing profession,
nurse and vet as we have seen; or both musicians, perhaps one a
pianist and one a composer, types that support and complete the

other. They might both be active in the new enlightening wave that is passing through the church, such as The Churches' Fellowship of Psychical Study in Great Britain. They might be impresarios, furthering the work of artists and innovators; perhaps they are publishers, alive to the responsibility of bringing new spiritual literature to the public. They might be teachers, social workers, or business persons, espousing ethics and responsibility in the business world. Whatever their field, it is sure to be a work of service. At their core they are artists and scientists, following one great stream or the other, and whichever of these it is, it is most likely the same one for both. The line could be indistinct: the artistic soul in a scientific profession, for the purpose of softening some of science's rigid positions; or the scientific soul in the artist, to create new dimensions in art.

Above all, twin souls are distinguishable by their ideal balance of masculine and feminine. The male is secure in his masculinity, yet with markedly developed feminine qualities; his female counterpart is strong in womanliness, exercising freely her masculine powers. Their powers are interchangeable. Yin and yang flow without obstruction between them, meeting the need of the moment in either one. Gender harmony arches supreme over all their compatibilities. Without it the twin souls would not yet have joined. Gender development has been the core purpose of their divided evolutionary path. Now it becomes the basic factor in their harmony.

And their harmony is such that no competition arises between them. If competition exists between a man and a woman, one can safely assume that they are not twin souls. The soul cannot compete with itself, one half fighting for supremacy over the other.

Twin-soul love is notable for its quality of harmlessness. There is no desire to hurt, no deliberate wounding, never a missile aimed at the other. For the twin souls the space between cause and effect virtually disappears; they are brought to simultaneity. Each feels the other's hurt almost before it is inflicted. Exquisite care is exercised that no pains but growing pains are allowed.

And there *are* growing pains. While twin souls are blessed with the state of consciousness that accompanies spiritual love, they remain entirely human. This means that imperfections are threaded through all the graces, the lower still tugs at the higher, and the lessons in this schoolroom of the Universe are not over.

The challenge for twin souls is to learn to fit together as separate persons within one soul. Their concordances are of the mind and spirit, while their variances are of the emotions. They are not exempt from the day-to-day difficulties of people with different upbringings and ingrained habit patterns. For all their basic harmony, they still clash at certain points.

A sequence is found in the conflict between parties; all of life is for growth, and human growth is fueled by the pattern of conflict and resolution. It is true that we grow in relationship. The clashes, therefore, are inevitable and part of the Plan. The clash heads toward climax and resolution. For some people it is a prolonged process, with great spans of time between clash and climax, or between climax and resolution. In those long stretches, hostilities grow, and the next step is delayed. This pattern is found in every human conflict, large or small, the largest being the wars between nations, the smallest, perhaps, the little scraps between children, followed by quick resolutions.

Twin souls have their own method in this. They travel express through the sequence, working busily toward the goal all the while. Anger and blame do not exist between them, thus the time between stages is used for honest exploration, individually and together. They are naturally committed to absolute honesty and unconditional love. Any tension is used for gaining deeper understanding and discovering the next needed step in their growth. There is little or no delay; they move swiftly from clash to climax to resolution and unfailingly create a new balance of forces.

Thus they mount the ladder of evolution at an accelerated pace, each resolution broadening their understanding of each other, creating closer communication and deepening their love. Every new perception brings into clearer focus the true being of the other, as Abraham Maslow has described it in his theory of B-cognition. It also points to the richness of being-love. Twin souls love the being of the other, which in a broad sense is the being of themselves. This is self-love in the truest sense: love of the divine essence within all things. With this most acute and penetrating type of perception the being-lover is able to discern realities in the beloved to which others are blind, including, perhaps, the beloved him or herself. Love is not blind; nonlove is blind. Real love is all-seeing. And in seeing the potential gifts in each other, the twins draw them forth into manifestation. Self-improvement, which has been the driving force within each, now includes improvement of the self-in-other.

Another way of recognizing the twinship of souls is by the amount of dark-force intervention in their lives—particularly if they have an urgent work of service to do. Deep emotional fears might be triggered, unexpectedly, at a high point of closeness and happiness, when all the future looks bright. Remember, the twins are at the tip of the pyramid—closest to the light and therefore closest to the dark. One of them may have hidden anxieties that otherwise would have lain dormant, perhaps for the remainder of the life—though always with an inhibiting effect on the life. The breadth and depth of the twin-soul feelings, as they sweep through the subconscious mind, work toward healing, the way a cathartic works on the body.

The conflict may be aggravated by surrounding circumstances. The stricken twin may, like Harriet Taylor, be struggling to resolve a "love" triangle. The triangle, of course, has its purifying purpose; but if all forces come together in collision, the twin-soul base can be shaken. It is here, at just this vulnerable point, that the dark forces release their poison-tipped arrows, subtly piercing the mind of the beleaguered one, creating shadows of doubt. The doubts take many forms, and are tailored to the emotional frailties of the person under siege. Among the devout, and even among the saints when under the pall, the form is frequently doubt in the existence of God. Doubt about oneself, doubt about the twin, and doubt about the twin soul principle itself are other forms.

Even worse, the insidious voices of the Separatists may affirm the principle, but pervert it. One example is that of the man who suddenly became seized with the idea that twin souls need not return to the other half of themselves, but could choose any other twin. There is no question that powers of Darkness are at the source of this distortion. They would like nothing better than for all the separated twins to be stirred up in confusion and no half ever find its true other half. Creation would cease absolutely, for none of the group unions could take place without the twins leading. The evil forces would be demolished, too, but they are willing to be kamikaze bombers; after all, they invented it.

This is to remind us that the arrival of the twin soul doesn't guarantee safety. It brings us much closer to it, but by way of enormous challenges. The fairy-tale dragons guarding the gate are born of this cosmic truth.

When the crisis comes, there is strong support from the twin. Further evidence of twinship is the unconditional love, which does not waver under fire. The twins will already have earned close friends who are part of their group soul. These will gather around with compassion and understanding, with new inner sources of love opened up by the suffering one, who after all is suffering for them. Their experience is shared experience. When the twin partners move back into the light, the light will be brighter over them all.

It is truly said that the dark angel can't reach to the top; but it can aim for the high souls on the way. The Path is a series of tests. There are plateaus for rest, but the tests never cease, and with ascension become more exacting. There may be mists of delusion, one mirage after another. For many, romantics especially, the mirages wear the as yet unknown face of the twin, and they may think their twin is found when it is not. Recognizing one's own creation is simple. There is no point in saying, 'When it is the twin I will know it.' We can as easily know it when it is not, and doubt it when it is.

The question "How can I ever be sure?" is not easily answered, because the recognition can be a long, slow process. Finally, when much evidence has accumulated and many tests have been passed together, only the most serious doubter fails to see the truth. Yet we can never be absolutely certain. We can only be certain of the love we feel, and the other can be certain of the love we show; ultimately that is what matters. In naming twin soulship we give ourselves a guide through the cosmic Plan. The *love* is the goal of the search, not the twin.

Martin Israel, a British parish priest, author, minister of healing and widely traveled retreat conductor, gives us these words of wisdom: "I feel that when people seek the Kingdom of God with their full being, much more will be added as well, including an encounter with their twin soul. Too much search for a twin soul could have selfish overtones, and divert one from doing one's work properly in the immediate future."

The twin meeting occurs, not as the result of a search, but when readiness is won. As for recognition, twin souls recognize in each other the ideal partner and can perfectly fulfill their love without knowledge of the principle. Undoubtedly there are many twin marriages on earth in which the partners have never even heard the term. Such a pair was Frank Tribbe and his beloved wife, Audre. He writes of her death, and through his simple description of their marriage reveals and delineates their twinship. They were not in their first youth when they came together. Both had been married before, and had endured many trials, tests that led to the meeting of the paths. Frank writes:

> If one word could adequately describe our marriage, for both of us, that word would be "fulfillment." For the greatest twenty-four years of my life, she was wife, lover, friend, and associate. Our interests, likes and dislikes, tastes and beliefs were as nearly identical as could be possible between two people. Our small disagreements we accepted without rancor, and "the sun never went down upon our wrath." We were almost totally compatible and our togetherness was always a subject of comment from others. We were together nearly twenty-five years, and our marriage of eighteen and a half years coincided with our retirement, so we were physically together almost every day for the entire period, and revelled in it. We enjoyed discussing every

subject under the sun, but could also take deep pleasure from hours of silence as we sat close. My Audre wouldn't even ride on the right side in our old Chrysler—she sat in the middle to be close to me, in spite of lack of padding and the stares from young people. The highlight of every day at home, for us both, was the evening, as Audre sat in the library reading or writing, while I worked at my desk or read in my lounger. Reading to each other was a special pleasure, as was watching a scene of nature. It's such a lonely world without her.

So when are we ready to meet our twin? How will we know that? We are ready when no longer needy, when we are strong and complete in ourselves, our masculine and feminine forces in balance.

Readiness comes through our inner work, and especially our work at learning of love, which indeed traces our steps toward the Kingdom of God. We need not have found the twin in order to practice being-love and being-cognition. Every person we meet has a true being hidden inside, and that being is worthy of love. Mother Teresa perceives and loves the true being in the world's most materially and physically disadvantaged people. We can't be Mother Teresa, but we can attempt to feel and act *as if* we were. Dr. Roberto Assagioli has written about the "as if" technique. Realizing, for instance, that we are not yet enlightened, we can try to behave *as if* we were, and in this way steer toward enlightenment. By the same token the attempt to follow the twin-soul model in relationships quickens our steps toward the twin.

We can, like the twins, strive to draw out the highest and finest in the other; we can locate and love the partner's true being; we can feel *as if* our souls are one—for in truth all souls are one. This is very different from "forcing the fit." The first is a realistic effort at self-betterment; the second is based on illusion.

We all have a tendency to idealize the love partner—until disillusionment sets in, turning us around the opposite way. The idealization is caused by our harboring deep in the soul the image of the ideal complement. We long for the perfect matching with the twin.

Our desire for completion is so great that we try to enact the twin marriage, deluding ourselves into believing that we have arrived. There is a natural impatience with the arduous work and snail's pace of our soul's evolution. We constantly strain forward, hoping we have attained a higher point than our labors allow.

And so, with our loves, we seize impatiently upon the ready partner and force the belief that the twin ideal has been met. In order to validate that belief, we often repress our true needs; the falsity is rationalized away. This is forcing the fit, and insofar as the fit is false, we, too, are false.

Others can see our falsity where we cannot. One needn't be a trained psychoanalyst to see through such dreams; but an analyst sees through them to specific causes. One man was in analysis for unrecognized problems. He had been married for many years and had fathered five children. All this time his wife had criticized and cruelly carped at him. The man reported her behavior, but showed no anger. The analyst heard instead an idealization of the woman and a repeated affirmation that she was always right. It became clear that the patient was agreeing with his wife's criticisms so that he could repress his hostility toward her. By making her perfect, he had no cause for anger and could continue in the illusion that he was happily married. In so doing he was delaying his progress in life, and hers as well—also that of the twin soul, who is affected in absentia.

Some time later, this man divorced and subsequently met his twin other. Five years afterward he reports that he is remarried and happily fulfilled. His story demonstrates the following of the fit, instead of its forcing.

And what about fleeing the fit? These are times when fear grips the heart and overrules it. The bachelor finds himself in love, but is afraid. He fears losing his independence; or he fears that he may not have found the true love, the ideal woman for him. He flees, rather than facing his anxiety, surmounting it, and giving his heart the opportunity to respond. Another example is the woman who has been hurt several times and becomes hostile to men altogether. When she meets a man who could genuinely love her she runs away from him. Her heart is caught in a grip of fear, fear of being hurt again. The fit is not followed; the heart is not allowed to open.

Another type of fleeing is a combination of forcing the fit and fleeing the fit. This occurs when a man or woman pursues the ideal image born of childhood experience. The growing boy sees the mother as a model for perfect love union. He carries her mental image subconsciously through life as he searches for a wife. Finally he thinks he has found the ideal woman, but if he sees the least blemish in her the picture is spoiled. He is forcing the fit by trying to force the childhood image of the mother on the present-day opportunity; he is fleeing the fit by looking for something that is the product of his memory and imagination. Thus it becomes impossible to find the true partner.

In a similar manner a woman may look for a man to fit the idealized image of her father. When she thinks she has found the perfect protector and giver of love, she is soon conflicted, for her vision was of the childhood ideal, the one who was and is unattainable.

Such complexes can be found at the root of a great many marriages. A typically confining case is the one in which two people marry young, have children, and then one outgrows the other. They remain locked in enforced, symbiotic union, neither free nor connected. One or both may then idealize the other in order to justify the union. They rationalize away their incompatibilities, which may in fact be so great as to produce monumental unhappiness and boredom. This is a forcing of the fit, and also, a fleeing of a true fit that may someday arise. At the same time it is a flight from the true self.

All of this is about recognizing ourselves. For we must first recognize and know ourselves before we can recognize our twin. When we stop following the false trails and stand still awhile, we may find that we are nearer to the real twin than we thought. We don't want to be like the man lost in a blizzard who was found dead of exposure just twenty yards from his home.

CHAPTER EIGHT

DANGERS IN THE NEW AGE

W HEN YOU do not see, say clearly, 'I do not see.' When you think you see, say clearly, 'I think I see.' When you are certain that you see, ask a wise person, 'What do *you* see?'"

These days many people seem very certain that they see. They see "spiritual truths," but in a light that is as likely to be false as true. When they ask a wise man what he sees, too often he is an impostor from unseen dimensions, or the product of their own imagination.

Such is the peril of an enlightened time. The pyramid, with a conjunction of the light and the dark at its tip, may be applied symbolically to world movements, as well as to the individual. We are on the edge of breakthrough to the light of a spiritual renaissance. As guiding forces gather to bring about the birth, their shadow counterpart trails closely, with the determined aim of aborting it.

In the end it will be seen that the shadow has assisted the birth and given richness to the light, but only by means of the struggle between them. Therefore, we must enter the struggle. In entering it with clear sight, we will help fulfill its purpose and add our portion to raising the happiness level of the world.

Nature, with her cunning ways, turns the rabbit's coat to white in wintertime to conceal it against the snow. In a similar move of self-preservation, the Prince of Darkness has donned new raiment for this New Age.

We are accustomed to seeing evil as a clear-cut menace, dark-visaged, easily distinguishable from good. When it steps onto the world stage, as it has several times in this century, the world rises up collectively, ready to fight it to the finish. When it appears in society with obvious devilish intent, it meets with laws enacted to counter the threat. Under these circumstances, the dark face of evil has allure only for those who themselves live in its shade. Others, who walk in sunlight, can see the approaching shadow.

A recognizable dark force can be combatted. But what are we to do when evil comes robed in light? This is the light of the false sun, the light that blinds. It throws stardust in our eyes and we lose direction. We are steered from our true goal to a substitute, one that is artificial and ultimately self-destructive.

Rudolf Steiner has given names to the two guises of evil: Lucifer, the light and fantastically airborne; and Ahriman, the heavy, dark, and down-pulling. Lucifer and Ahriman work in tandem, keeping humanity off balance and so retarding its progress. Luciferan light works upon our best impulses; Ahrimanic shadow exploits our worst. Communism, for instance, with its fundamental idealism, was a Luciferan assignment. But once the grip of communism was established, Ahriman gained hold of it for the exercise of power, cruelty, and materialism. The Nazi terror was a pure manifestation of Ahriman. Periodically each takes center stage. Now, in the New Age, it is Lucifer's turn.

The New Age has created a near-perfect climate for his misleading light. The spiritual seeker tends to fall prey to illusion in a way that the average person does not. This is a time of spiritual searching such as our world has never known. People are desperate for light on the path. Countless numbers find that religion has failed them. They are bereft of faith, just at the time when a major evolutionary move is in force, inspiring a soul-hunger for upliftment and return to God.

Never has there been such a wonderful opportunity for the Luciferan forces to spread their dazzling light of illusion. Opportunists that they are, they create the impression that they are aiding the progress of souls while in truth they are retarding them in great numbers. If we could read their program mapped out in advance, which of course it was in nether realms, as was *Mein Kampf,* we would see listed first in their array of tools: Psychic Glamour.

Psychic glamour is the glamorizing of the spiritual search and of the seeker. The result is falsification and distortion, and a delay in progress that could be serious or even fatal to the soul. Under the bright cloud of psychic glamour the seeker becomes exalted, not to heights of the spirit but to the peaks of ego inflation. Whereas the spiritual goal is growth into reality, the glamoured soul sinks progressively into delusion. The essence of this delusion is that great progress is being achieved; whereas in fact, the opposite is true and the soul is captive.

The feelings inspired by the condition are enticing. Psychic glamour is the stuff of romance. It is to spirituality what romantic love is to soul love; it is high excitement and thrill; it sees the world through technicolored glasses; it makes one feel singled out, set apart and above. This exaltation closely imitates spiritual joy. Those in its grip do not doubt; they *know.* They cannot be reached by voices of reason—as parents of cult victims can attest.

How do we distinguish between psychic glamour and true spiritual inspiration? The one is characterized by pride, the other by humility. The one demands easy answers and quick returns, the other accepts with patience and courage the demands of the arduous climb, finding joy in the upliftment of others rather than the self.

The agents of psychic glamour come from the astral plane, both the lower and higher levels. Their first requirement is that their victims cast aside critical judgment. The mind of the person under siege becomes subtly influenced, believing that the abdicating of will is a surrender to God.

A typical beginning is this: a person who is psychically open and has aspirations makes contact with an astral spirit, directly or through a medium. A deficiency in the person, perhaps a weak sense of self, meets with the fantasies and ambitions of the entity itself, and as a result the person gains feelings of specialness and grandeur. There is a sense of expansion and a new state of being. Emotions are stirred, and there may even be feelings of love.

133

All this is interpreted as spiritual upliftment and may induce excitement, feverish joy, a profound conviction that spiritual transformation has occurred. Such sensations are mere imitations of the true ecstasy that accompanies soul union. The deluded seeker may become wrapped in a cocoon of sanctimonious bliss, fancying the self as the reincarnation of Saint Joan, a prophet, or a pharaoh—fantasies abundantly provided from the Luciferan cornucopia. The past lives always depict people of greatness, never an obscure barber or farmer. And whatever messages come through to the fevered brain are accepted unquestioningly.

The glamorized seeker is first sent soaring into the sun on wings of wax … then the instructions begin. They may come from a direct inner voice or through such psychic tools as the pendulum, the Ouija board, automatic writing, or a medium's transmissions. The victim begins to be told what to do.

Victims tend to be sensitive, willing, open, and trusting. They have probably been much exploited by others. They are also needy. Feeling attended to and cared for in the situation, specially chosen over the heads of others, they will do what they are told.

The operative word here is "told." "I was told by the spirits to…" For example, a widow was told that she must sell her house and move to a cabin in the woods, there to do great works of art for the world. Obediently she listed her house with a realtor. The market was down, and the house did not sell. She was told to cut the price by half. She did, and soon sold her house. Before moving to the isolated cabin to which she had been directed, she decided to have her teeth attended to, since they were giving her trouble. She was told to do nothing; the trouble would right itself. Again, she obeyed. In the end she lost her teeth, and she lost the small amount of money remaining from her house sale as she sat waiting for the great works to materialize. They never did.

People who normally do not let anyone tell them what to do, not their mother, or their spouse, or their children, will nevertheless turn over the management of their lives to invisible forces in worlds they have never seen! Such is the power of delusion. It should be added that the widow was well educated and had been a successful artist before her spirit was broken. Extreme as the incident may sound, it is typical of a glamour that has ruined many lives. People have been "told" of buried treasure in Egypt and have set off, directions in hand, to dig it up. Others have been told of a twin soul in a distant land and have followed the path lit by Luciferan light to inevitable ruin.

There is another ray of Luciferan light that is less easily recognized. It shines on the serious spiritual seekers who are under the thrall of channeled teachings. These are people who would not think of taking dictation from a spirit in the conduct of their practical affairs, yet eagerly surrender the control of their inner lives to untested entities.

The deceptions that we have considered are the work of gleeful or unevolved spirits on the lower astral plane. On somewhat higher astral levels are a multitude of other spirits with a little occult knowledge and aspirations toward teaching. Human ambitions live on in the afterworld. When combined with astral deception they can rebound with potent effect.

The desire for learning is strong in the human soul. The soul desires above all to learn the nature of itself, its origin, and its Creator. It craves knowledge of the universal purpose and its own part in the Plan. The force that would exploit that desire and turn it to the service of evil, namely the frustration of the Divine Plan, is diabolical indeed.

With the natural speeding up of evolution at this time, suggestible persons are easily convinced that they must find a shortcut to learning. Not good enough are the old ways of acquiring spiritual knowledge: apprenticeship with a guru, who first impresses on his students the immense labor demanded in the ascent; years of inner work; the gradual purification of body and mind; studies of the ancient wisdom; and always, as an accompaniment, growth through service.

The new way is to head straight for the top, borne aloft by "great teachers" from the beyond. These teachers express themselves through selected human beings, who channel their words in an atmosphere of hushed reverence. It is claimed that they speak from exalted realms of the spirit; and so there is imparted a strong implication of special status for the listeners, and even more for the channeling medium. Pride enters subtly. Considerable attention is paid to the ego and personality of the entity, though always behind a veil of modesty. Plainly much "channeled" material originates in the mind of the channeler, and the tribute paid is to the channeler!

Where psychics are actually taken over by spirits claiming to be highly evolved beings, we may be fairly sure that these are astral pretenders. Not all such entities are deliberately fraudulent, but may deceive themselves as to their stature. Many such beings crowd round the earth plane, entities from various levels of astral existence, their work spanning conscious destructiveness to higher impulses carried over from human life. In a past human life they themselves may have been unwitting channels for low-caliber teachings.

Advanced teachers *do* exist in the spiritual worlds. However, they do not use the voices of intermediaries. They inspire the intuitional minds of the truly wise here in our midst, teachers such as Martin Israel and Omraam Aivanhov, both of whom state their ideas as their own. Men like these neither shirk the responsibility for them nor congratulate themselves as chosen messengers. Their books carry their own name and not that of an exotic spirit, their writings stand up to close scrutiny and discriminating judgment, quite unlike most of the channeled output.

The tremendously popular channeled works crowding the metaphysical bookstores are, for the most part, innocuous and platitudinous. They are curiously alike and of a pattern, repeating in pretentious language what has often been said before. Their harm lies in their capacity to delay the progress of those held in their thrall. Their central appeal is the promise of ascension that short-circuits the very real need for serious study, hard work, and service to others, which constitute the only path to the development of the self. Such writings seldom instruct in meditation, nor do they recommend the classics of spiritual literature. They offer no guidance in the disciplines needed for becoming one's own channel to higher wisdom.

Such a course would, after all, obviate the necessity for the dictating entity and the paid channeler.

The superior status accorded channeled works is part of the romantic myth. All inspiration, good or evil, is channeled from unseen worlds. Beethoven channeled his symphonies from the exalted planes of musical creation, in collaboration with his own higher Self. Brahms on his deathbed cried out, "The works were not mine, the works were not mine!" He was co-creator in the right sense. He fulfilled the purpose of his life by endowing the world with masterpieces formed of his unique essence in conjunction with high inspiration. It is the same with the creative writer working in conscious partnership with his or her muse. This contrasts with the automatic writer, who is merely an automaton, the undiscriminating tool of a passing entity.

New revelation is trying to make its way into the world at this time. It strives to contact the high Self of aspiring individuals who have lifted themselves by their own labor, through the development of love, will and intuition. When the genuinely advanced beings who guide our destinies locate a clear channel to humanity, they use it abundantly. In their view the human instrument is more than an instrument: it is a participating intelligence. Alice Bailey and H.P. Blavatsky are outstanding examples. In relaying the teachings of the Tibetan masters, they did not channel in today's sense: they transmitted. They remained fully conscious and in control of their own excellent minds. They worked in partnership with their teachers, on the mental and intuitional planes, and were regarded with respect as true aspirants and as masters of their true selves.

One of the books written by the Tibetan master, Djwhal Khul, with Alice Bailey is titled: *Glamour: A World Problem*. The problem of glamour was foreseen to be of worldwide dimension, affecting a broader spectrum than that which we have been considering here. The tidal wave of psychic glamour has a retarding effect on the whole of society because it creates a separation between spiritual seekers and those who have not yet consciously begun their search. The conventional person looks at the flakey happenings all around and wants no part of them. True spirituality becomes suspect by association.

Conventional people represent the next wave in the forward flow. That wave is delayed by the craziness tainting the first. Besides, it is likely that the conventional man or woman, busy with useful work in the world, is more highly evolved than those with their heads in the clouds and feet off the ground.

This raises another question: "How evolved am I?" Spiritual pride goes along with the prevailing mood of psychic glamour. The question could be answered this way: The more highly evolved we are, the lower we see ourselves on the scale of that which is yet to be attained. And the converse is true.

Alice Bailey, in *From Intellect to Intuition,* asks the pertinent question: "How can one distinguish between the truly inspired writings of the true knower, and this mass of literature which is flooding the minds of the public at this time?" And she answers:

> First, I should say that the true inspirational writing will be entirely without self-reference; it will sound a note of love…; it will convey definite knowledge and carry a note of authority by its appeal to the intuition; it will respond to the law of correspondences, and fit into the world picture; above all, it will carry the impress of Divine Wisdom and lead the race on a little further. As to its mechanics, the writers of such a type of teaching will have a real understanding of the methods they employ. They will have mastered the technique of the process; they will be able to guard themselves from illusion, and from the intrusion of personalities, and will have a working knowledge of the apparatus with which they are working. If they are receiving teachings from discarnate entities, and from great Masters, they will know how to receive it, and will then know all about the agent transmitting the teaching.

As great numbers of people are led into blind alleys and backwaters of the spirit by Luciferan light, the forces of Ahriman have their own contributions to make. They will meet up with Lucifer in many places. A typical way in which the two faces of evil collude is the luring of innocents into the camps of the false gurus, and the imposition of dominance and cruelty once they are there.

Where does our susceptibility to these forces begin? We believe that it begins in early childhood. There is a phase in the early development of the child called the anal phase. Occurring between the ages of one and a half to two and a half, it is a time when the child is preoccupied with power. He is able to control his bowels and bladder, a circumstance that provides the child with a feeling of power—not only over his bodily eliminations but over his parents. It is a time when the child can truly say no and thus deny others. The struggle between the child and the parents blends with sadistic and cruel impulses. The child basks in the glory of standing upright, of walking, of gaining the omnipotence provided by the use of words. All of these provide a sense of great power.

We know from those who have had the stimulation of too much anal struggle at this stage of life that they become preoccupied with the infliction of punishment. Those who have had too many enemas become filled with rage and cruelty. If the personality retains considerable fixation at this stage of life, albeit covered over with more mature manifestations of the personality, the propensity to cruelty and power-seeking remains. This opens a door for the forces of Ahriman, and thus for the societies and the people who are attracted to black magic, sadism, and the possession of others through the wielding of power.

Emotional factors are present also on the Luciferan side. The entities assigned to this work are spurred on by a strong element of jealousy—jealousy of people who may be "more good," more enlightened, more spiritual than they could hope to become. Their effectiveness springs from a jealous desire to impede the spiritually inclined and bring them down to their level. The same manifestations appear in certain personalities. There is jealousy of those who have more in the way of possessions and personal gifts. Such characteristics derive from childhood sibling rivalry, as well as the desire to be "guru in the Light," to have people admire and worship them, pay tribute to them, clothe them in glamour.

What protection do we have against falling under the sway of these appealing influences? One is to look inward when their effect begins to play upon us, and recognize, if we can, our emotional responses, and what they might be signifying in the way of self-satisfaction. Another is to use our God-given critical faculties to discriminate between the true and the false. The astral experience is part of our learning, a terrain that must be crossed, but as quickly as possible to avoid getting stuck. We can work to maintain a healthy skepticism, resolving to examine everything in the light of our own judgment. One should accept nothing—the words in these pages included—unless confirmed by one's own intuition and common sense.

The question arises: Where is the God of Goodness while all this evil is going on? The God of Goodness is at the center of everything, the evil and the good, which, taken together, add up to a wholeness of good far beyond human grasp. The higher mind, the true Self, from its position above the duality of existence, is able to know the perfection of the Plan, and its single purpose, which is Joy.

Before the original separation, the divine Joy was all. The separation was for the expansion of Joy through calling back to Itself the ever-expanding souls born of Its consciousness. Duality was created for this, that the separated halves would struggle toward reunion and transfiguration. Good as we know it, limited and partial, was created for this, with its opposite partner, evil, dancing the dance of life in its arms. Masculine and feminine were created for this, divided for this, urged toward reunion for this through sexual attraction, the divine gift of Love. Recovery of the original Joy is the goal of all striving, above and below, from the beginning to the end, to reimmersion in the Godhead, which is God and Goddess, He and She, thou and I writ large.

Then shall the perfection be seen! It is perceptible now behind the slow crawl of the world, the race of atoms, each one accounted for, each in its place, alike to the placement of souls in their great reassembling. Even as we look at the dangers, quietly the hidden secret stirs: all is secure. There is no portion but is made of goodness and mercy. The missteps of the few are the gift of learning to the many. The fallen and the lifted-up alike will be taken back, and in the Wholeness made whole.

And That which made the beautiful earth is making it ready to receive its twin lovers. Across its breadth they approach each other, their steps numbered, by the same perfect design as the greater return that they reflect. Their footsteps are monitored by angels. When the exact count is reached, the twin souls will appear to each other's sight at the place designated.

How will their lives conjoin? The matter is perfectly simple for Those who direct the traffic of the Universe. It was all set in motion with the first breath of God, and each moving part involving every other throughout the infinitude of cosmic dimensions is keyed to receive the signal when it comes; and oceans will part and mountains move and the affairs of men stand still to make way for two hands outstretched at the moment of their time.

APPENDIX

QUESTIONS & ANSWERS

Q: Most people are not married to their twin soul. How do they reconcile themselves to that fact, once they hear about the beauties of twinship?

A: Knowing about the beauties of twinship should help the present relationship by encouraging the partners to hold each other lightly, not graspingly; for they are only lent to one another, as our children are lent to us for a time. They are not ours to keep. We have had other children and other marriages in former lives, and will have still others again. All of them are for the purpose of teaching us better how to love. A marriage that is not a twin marriage can be very happy and inspiring, as the participants realize that they are on a journey and not at a fixed point. By helping each other on the journey, they can form a spiritual partnership with the same commitment as that of the twins: to assist each other's spiritual growth. The joys can be comparable in that way, and in many others that will emerge from that central core.

Q: Do twin souls have separate karmas?

A: The karma they have been living, each separately, has been a preparation for their coming together in twinship. Thereafter their karmas are intertwined. It's rather like two lines approaching each other, similar to railroad tracks converging in the distance. In that convergence the separate karmas meet. The lines do not fuse, but they run parallel and very close. From then on they may be thought of as sharing a joint karma. As for the individual karmic debts that they brought with them to the union, they will help each other to discharge these, just as the burden of monetary debt would be shouldered together in a good marriage. Similarly they will share the joy of each other's karmic credits. The inexplicable happiness that falls over the one may stem directly from the past deeds of the other, who is, after all, the other side of self.

It must be remembered, too, that throughout their long journey back together, whatever happened to either one had its reverberations in the other, much as occurs in lesser degree between every created soul and every other. Twin souls are responsible for each other in a way that is closer, though not different, from the manner in which we are all responsible for one another. At root there is no such thing as separate karma, only degrees of the joy or pain that follow from our choices.

Q: I'm sure my husband and I are twin souls. But I can't tell him that, because he doesn't believe in these things. Is it possible for one twin to be more highly evolved than the other?

A: No. Twins evolve at approximately the same rate, one moving a little ahead of the other, then drawing the other forward, in more or less alternating fashion. When they meet, they are level; they will not meet otherwise. But the leveling is a matter of soul growth. There can be disparities in psychological development. One twin could have mental barriers, resistances against certain types of knowledge to which the other twin is party. Elizabeth Barrett Browning believed in spiritualism, and Robert did not. What your husband consciously believes is of little importance as long as he is the true and good man you describe. *That* is the measure of evolution.

Q: I get the impression that the twin-soul relationship is first, and every other union is second, or third, or fourth, or way down the line.

A: That is a human impression. In the broader spiritual dimension there is no such count. To Him who sees the littlest sparrow fall, the sparrow is first, equal with the highest angel. In the realm of Reality, every relationship of love is first. To value it as first, to treat it in your life as first, is to sanctify it with the same divine aura that encompasses the reunited twins.

Q: One channeling teacher has stated that Jesus and Mary were twin souls. Do you think this is likely?

A: No. Incestuous implications would attach to a twin soul connection within the family context. We feel certain that on this account twins never incarnate as parent and child or brother and sister. The union of twin souls is a love union in the fullest sense; with reason, they have been termed "the Immortal Lovers." They are mates, finely fashioned vehicles for the sexual polarities. It is a different category entirely from Jesus and Mary. Moreover, the characters of Jesus and Mary, as they come down to us, contain nothing of those attributes that signify the matching and complementing of twin souls.

Q: Is there not a danger of reaching for a partner in the hope he or she may prove to be the twin?

A: Every reach of man toward woman and woman toward man is motivated at soul level by the hope of finding the twin. So it has been for every move toward love throughout the ages. Now that conscious knowledge of twin soulship is coming into our possession, it is no different, except in this: we can begin to know the specific, identifying features that signify the true twin matching, so that when the long-lost other of the self is found, we will realize it and so experience the happiness more profoundly, as is always the case when unconscious knowledge is made conscious. And knowing this, we will be better able to counter the inevitable opposition from dark forces.

Q: If Plato gave our first image of twin souls—in the hermaphrodite divided into its male and female halves—how did the term "platonic love" come to be accepted as sexless?

A: Intelligent human beings have always longed for a love greater than earthly love alone, a love that admits of the spirit. The idea of the two separated halves, searching for each other through the vastness of time, speaks to the soul of its own predicament. Platonic love came closest to the promise of fulfillment. Yet the limitation of the human mind has made it unable to conceptualize the whole picture. We need a new definition of platonic love. Platonic love, in its true sense, means the love of the whole being, not excluding the sexuality of the human state but elevating it to transcendent expression.

Q: The recorded cases of cosmic consciousness show that the average age of illumination is in the early thirties. Is there a usual age at which twin souls are likely to meet?

A: From the limited knowledge that we now have, there does not appear to be any rule of age for twin-soul meetings. Twins may find each other when advanced in years and recognize the youthful spirit in one another as no one else can; or they may meet as children. In one case a boy and girl of five—with matching first names, one feminized—were brought together by their parents. After one look, the children went and put their arms around each other. For years they played together in perfect harmony and devotion; then a family move put an ocean between them. Some years later they met again, and their bond continued exactly as it had left off. Everything about them

145

pointed to twinning. We don't yet know the outcome of this story, but an eventual marriage and life of fulfillment seems likely.

Twin souls can meet in every conceivable circumstance and combination of ages. We know of an instance where the woman was middle-aged, an advanced teacher and sage. One of her students was a young doctor, headed for renown himself. After her death, he devoted his life to promoting and expanding her teachings. These were very likely twin souls, and their reunion was primarily one of service—and, of course, further growth for both of them through service.

We do believe, however, that as the New Age progresses, twin souls will be reuniting in large numbers at marriageable age. The Plan is surely that they shall establish a new kind of marriage, soul-marriage fully realized on the physical plane, with family harmony hitherto unknown on this warring earth.

Then will wars be prevented at the source. Only then shall we see the significance in the words of Swedenborg: "Those who are truly married on earth are in heaven one angel."

Q: How can you support this idea, the most anti-feminist I've ever heard of, that a woman is so tied to a man that if his soul falls hers will too, and there's nothing she can do about it?

A: If one soul falls, the twin has everything to do with it. It is not that one twin goes down and drags the other down with him or her. Their evolution to this point has been an equal effort, each influencing the other, despite all distance. If one is tipped downward through some crucial choice, the other may choose to break the fall through a counter-choice or become a willing participant in the error. It is choice all the way, and neither one makes the choices for the other. They both possess free will. Twin souls are less inclined than any other kind of partners to impose their will on one another. Their ascent has been in tandem; if they fall it will be by mutual decision. They rise or fall together, for they are one. This is why, in twin souls, there is a great sense of responsibility for each other. It is like responsibility for the self.

Q: I am a woman this time. I firmly believe that I have lived before as a man. This has been confirmed by psychics. How can I correlate this with the idea of twin souls, each of them always incarnating as the same sex?

A: If we accept the principle of twin soulship, and not everyone will, we may be prepared to believe that our sense of having lived in the body of the opposite gender is emotionally based. Psychics who reinforce our convictions may be intuiting our own unconscious desires. There is good reason for the long-held belief that we change sexes with our incarnations. We know that the soul must gain the experience of both energies in the course of its evolution. It is a logical assumption that the energies will alternate with succeeding lives. But the laws of the soul are beyond logic. They are revealed to us gradually over time, and each new revelation tests our flexibility. At present there is a massive thought-form hovering over us from the astral plane: the certainty that we have lived in the body of both sexes. Fixed beliefs exist in every field of human thought; they are necessary for their time, and account for the resistance that inevitably meets fresh ideas. As new light makes its way into individual minds, outworn thought-forms evaporate. We believe that this will happen with the certainty about the sex-transfer of the incarnating soul. Even now we encounter women who say with conviction, "I *know* I was never a man." The same is true for some men, those who are secure in their soul identity. There could not be the longing of one twin for the other, the great need for the soul's completion through union with its opposite, unless the two halves rested upon the unvarying base of Eternal Feminine and Eternal Masculine.

*This book is set in Garamond, a standard
typeface used by book designers and printers
for four centuries, and one of the finest old styles
ever cut. Some characteristics of Garamond
to note are the small spur on the "G", the open
bowl on the "P", the curving tail on the "R",
and the short lower-case height and very
small counters of the "a" and "e".*

*The text stock is
55 lb. Windsor High-bulk Cream*

PRINTED IN CANADA BY
Friesen Printers